Y0-BVN-124

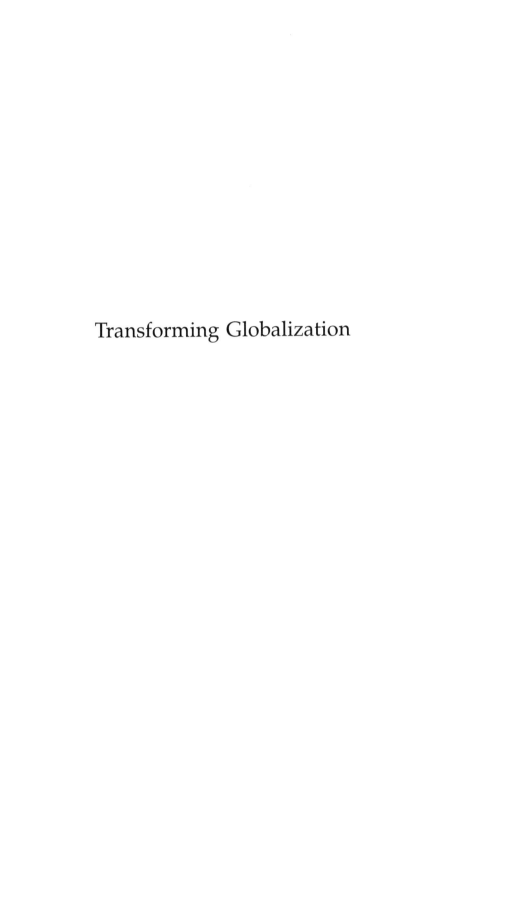

Transforming Globalization

Studies in Critical Social Sciences

Series Editor

DAVID FASENFEST
College of Urban, Labor and Metropolitan Affairs
Wayne State University

Editorial Board

JOAN ACKER, Department of Sociology, University of Oregon

ROSE BREWER, Afro-American and African Studies, University of Minnesota

VAL BURRIS, Department of Sociology, University of Oregon

CHRIS CHASE-DUNN, Department of Sociology, University of California-Riverside

G. WILLIAM DOMHOFF, Department of Sociology, University of California-Santa Cruz

COLLETTE FAGAN, Department of Sociology, Manchester University

MARTHA GIMENEZ, Department of Sociology, University of Colorado, Boulder

HEIDI GOTTFRIED, CULMA, Wayne State University

KARIN GOTTSCHALL, Zentrum für Sozialpolitik, University of Bremen

BOB JESSOP, Department of Sociology, Lancaster University

RHONDA LEVINE, Department of Sociology, Colgate University

JACKIE O'REILLY, WZB, Berlin

MARY ROMERO, School of Justice Studies, Arizona State University

CHIZUKO UENO, Department of Sociology, University of Tokyo

VOLUME 2

Transforming Globalization

Challenges and Opportunities in the Post 9/11 Era

Edited by

Bruce Podobnik & Thomas Reifer

HM
881
.G558
2005
West

BRILL

LEIDEN • BOSTON

2005

This book is printed on acid-free paper.

Library of Congress Cataloging-in-Publication Data

Transforming Globalization. Challenges and Opportunities in the Post 9/11 Era / edited by Bruce Podobnik & Thomas Reifer.
    p. cm. — (Studies in critical social sciences, ISSN 1573-4234; 3)
    Includes bibliographical references and index.
    ISBN 90-04-14583-4 (alk. paper)
    1. Social movements. 2. Anti-globalization movement. I. Podobnik, Bruce, 1968- II. Reifer, Thomas Ehrlich. III. Series.

HM881.G558 2005

2005047116

ISSN 1573-4234
ISBN 90 04 14583 4

© Copyright 2005 by Koninklijke Brill NV, Leiden, The Netherlands.
Koninklijke Brill NV incorporates the imprints Brill Academic Publishers,
Martinus Nijhoff Publishers and VSP.

All rights reserved. No part of this publication may be reproduced, translated stored
in a retrieval system, or transmitted in any form or by any means, electronic,
mechanical, photocopying, recording or otherwise, without prior written
permission from the publisher.

Authorization to photocopy items for internal or personal use is granted by
Koninklijke Brill NV provided that the appropriate fees are paid directly to
The Copyright Clearance Center, 222 Rosewood Drive, Suite 910,
Danvers, MA 01923, USA.
Fees are subject to change.

PRINTED IN THE NETHERLANDS

Contents

Bruce Podobnik and Thomas Reifer

The Effort to Transform Globalization: Historical and Contemporary Struggles

Throughout the history of the modern world-system, globalization projects promoted by global elites have been met with resistance from people on the ground whose livelihoods and security were threatened. As the geographic scale of global capitalism and state networks has expanded, and its penetration into daily life has deepened, the scale and intensity of resistance to this system has grown as well. Local efforts to protect traditional ways of life have evolved into national campaigns for union protections, and then into international movements for peace, social justice, and environmental sustainability.

Today, as global elites push for the final incorporation of all regions into a single capitalist system based on neoliberal principles, they are being met by an unexpectedly resilient, far-reaching, and multi-faceted coalition of resistance. Whatever it may be called – the 'anti-globalization movement,' the 'global solidarity movement,' or the 'globalization protest movement' – it is clear that a new coalition has emerged to challenge the dominance of political and corporate elites all across the contemporary world.

This book is dedicated to examining the modern characteristics and prospects of this coalition of resistance to elite-driven forms of globalization. We have gathered studies that explore various facets of the contemporary protest movement. While the authors draw on different theoretical traditions and make use of distinct methodologies, their central research questions are the same: What are the contemporary roots of various components of this anti-systemic movement? What beneficial synergies and/or tensions currently exist between constituent groups within the movement? And what are the future prospects of the protest movement? By providing a collection of studies that approaches these common questions from different perspectives, this book hopes to significantly advance our understanding of what is probably the most important progressive movement of our current era.

Because the chapters examine dynamics of opposition to state-corporate globalization in the contemporary period, we thought it appropriate to briefly sketch out in this introduction some of the earlier antecedents to this movement. It strike us as useful to compare and contrast dynamics of resistance in the first (late nineteenth century) and second (late twentieth century) major phases of financial globalization to have swept through the world-economy.[1] The articles in this book focus on dynamics of contestation in the second phase of globalization. But there are useful insights to be gained by looking back at forms of resistance that emerged in the earlier era as well.

If we examine the period from 1870–1914, when the world-system went through a particularly intense phase of financial globalization that was en-twined with interstate militarization, we find that a surprisingly rich array of transnational social movements were already contesting elite-driven projects. Undoubtedly the most important anti-systemic movement during this era was the labor movement. Not only were workers throughout Europe and North America mobilizing to form unions at the national level, but they were also forging impressive transnational organizations as well.

Indeed, the formation of the First International in 1864 revealed that European workers were attuned to the need to organize on an international level from a very early period. The resiliency of this transnational movement was demonstrated when, after the collapse of the First International, it was replaced by a Second International that was even broader in size and scope. From 1889 to 1914, the Second International exerted considerable ideological influence

---

[1] For more complete analyses of the world-historical roots of globalization protests, readers are encouraged to consult the following sources: Walton and Seddon (1994), Keck and Sikkink (1998), Silver and Slater (1999), and Boswell and Chase-Dunn (2000). See Chase-Dunn, Kawano, and Brewer (2000) for a presentation of new evidence regarding successive waves of trade globalization.

throughout Europe – and even supported worker's campaigns in North America and some other regions.

In addition to the consolidation of a transnational labor movement, this period also witnessed the emergence of a variety of international human-rights organizations and movements for global peace. Leading advocates for women's rights from Europe and North America, for instance, came together in 1888 to found the International Council of Women. This organization not only demanded equality in legal and political realms, but it also pushed for improvements in working conditions experienced by women and children. Soon afterward, one of the first international human-rights organizations, the Congo Reform Association, was formed to publicize depredations occurring in the rubber industry of the Belgian Congo. By mounting effective media and legal campaigns in Europe and the United States, the association was able to bring about important reforms in the colonial administration of the Congo. Peace activists also organized at both national and international levels, but obviously were unable to prevent the outbreak of World War I.

The period 1870–1914 also witnessed the emergence of international conservation associations dedicated to protecting specific species and ecosystems from commercial exploitation. Nature reserves have a long history in Europe, but the modern conservation movement really took shape in the 1870s with the institution of a national park system in the United States. Similar administrative systems, containing some prohibitions against com-mercial enterprise, then spread through other parts of the core before the First World War. Efforts were also undertaken to protect certain environmental resources in colonial areas during this period. The creation of the Convention for the Preservation of Wild Species in Africa in 1900, and the formation of the Society for the Preservation of the Wild Fauna of the Empire in 1903, are examples of this embryonic international environmental movement.

Labor, human rights, peace and conservation activists forged impressive transnational associations at the turn of the twentieth century. However, these organizations had important vulnerabilities that contemporary analysts would do well to note. Most significantly, virtually all the transnational organizations of that era were headquartered in core countries. And though many worked to address concerns of peoples in Asia, Africa, and Latin America, these organizations were nevertheless dominated by European and North American activists. Consequently, there were paternalistic and racist tendencies within many nineteenth century transnational organizations that limited their expansion into the colonial world. For these reasons, the transnational organizations that arose during the first major wave of financial globalization remained vulnerable to disruptions that swept through the core of the world-economy.

While many of these transnational organizations collapsed under the pressures of two world wars and a great depression, they nevertheless left enduring legacies. Through the successes they achieved, late nineteenth century workers, human rights, peace activists, and conservationists demonstrated that both capitalist firms and states could be confronted on a transnational level. Moreover, they created organizational tactics and cultures of opposition that remain important in many parts of the world. And, through their demise, they highlighted a crucial challenge that must be met by the contemporary globalization protest movement. Their example demonstrates that a movement of opposition to contemporary state-corporate globalization must be deeply rooted in all zones of the world-system, if it is to be truly enduring and egalitarian.

The second intense phase of state-corporate globalization, which has accelerated from the end of the Second World War to the present, has been accompanied by a movement of resistance that coalesced first in the developing world – and has since matured into an anti-systemic force of global proportions. The early manifestations of this movement came in the form of wide-ranging waves of anti-colonial and nationalist activism that swept through the periphery and semi-periphery from the late 1940s through the late 1970s.[2] Although these movements were rooted in specific countries, they also often generated regional associations and networks of mutual support. By the late 1970s, these anti-colonial and nationalist movements had brought about important trans-formations in the political and economic relations of power between elites in the global north and south.

Anti-colonial and nationalist movements were soon subjected to counter-offensives from domestic and international sponsors of neoliberal globalization policies. The re-assertion of a neoliberal form of globalization, spearheaded by the Reagan and Thatcher administrations, involved not only the intensifica-tion of military attacks against dissident governments and peoples, but also the imposition of increasingly severe austerity and deregulation policies throughout the developing world. The pressure exerted by the US and UK,

---

[2] Analyses of anti-colonial and nationalist movements of resistance can be found in: Girvan (1976), Bergquist (1986), and Cooper (1996).

as well as multi-lateral institutions such as the International Monetary Fund, the World Bank, and the General Agreement on Tariffs and Trade, succeeded in rolling back some nationalist and regulationist initiatives. However, structural adjustment policies also generated widespread protests from citizens throughout Asia, Africa, Latin America, and Eastern Europe.

Into the mid 1990s, dynamics of contestation between proponents and opponents of neoliberal forms of globalization and militarization were centered in the periphery and semi-periphery. However, by 1994 a new round of trade negotiations was bringing increased scrutiny to policies that protected key industries in core nations as well. As pressures to liberalize core economies grew, so too did defensive reactions from workers, farmers, and environ-mentalists in North America, Western Europe, and East Asia. By the mid 1990s, relatively new national and transnational activist networks headquartered in the global north began establishing links with more established, mature organizations centered in the global south. As a result, just as proponents of a neoliberal form of state-corporate globalization intensified their efforts to apply their policies on a world-scale, they were met by a multi-faceted coalition of resistance that was also capable of mounting actions on a global level.

The articles in this book investigate the recent evolution and current characteristics of this coalition of resistance. In terms of temporal coverage, the articles focus on the period from the 1970s onward – which is when those phenomena characteristic of contemporary globalization took off in a major way.

In his chapter "From 'Anti-Globalization' to the Global Justice Movement: Framing Collective Action Against Neoliberalism," Jeffrey Ayres explores the important conceptual and ideological work that has been done to define the agenda of the protest coalition. Jackie Smith, meanwhile, analyzes the growth and impact of the transnational social movement organizations that are part of the anti-globalization coalition. Her chapter, "Exploring Connections Between Global Integration and Political Mobilization," carries out an empirical analysis of the characteristics and orientations of these organizations in the contemporary period.

Bruce Podobnik's contribution, "Resistance to Globalization: Cycles and Trends in the Globalization Protest Movement," then offers a quantitative analysis of the broad characteristics of the protests. By conducting a content-analysis of news reports, he is able to show that the movement has grown into a remarkably diverse coalition that has been able to remain resilient in the post-9/11 period. Lesley Wood then focuses on a specific type of protest strategy that has been used in the movement. Her chapter, "Taking to the Streets Against Neoliberalism: Global Days of Action and Other Strategies," examines the historical and organizational roots of internationally-coordinated protests that were carried out between 1998 and 2001.

Gianpaolo Baiocchi's chapter, "The Workers' Party and the World Social Forum: Challenges of Building a Just Social Order," looks at two intriguing developments in Brazil. The election of the leader of the Workers' Party, Lula da Silva, to the Presidency, has brought a party with deep social movements roots into power. This is generating both hope and frustration, as efforts are undertaken to transform politics at the national level. At the same time, the World Social Forum has emerged as perhaps the most significant arena in which to re-imagine grassroots politics at the international level. In examining these developments, Baiocchi raises important questions about how new relations between parties and social movements might be created in the contemporary period.

Thomas Hall and James Fenelon then offer an exploration of the historical roots and contemporary dynamics of indigenous resistance. In "Trajectories of Indigenous Resistance Before and After 9/11," they argue that recent events like the terrorist attacks of September 11, 2001, are blips on the radar lying on top of a much deeper process of global capitalist expansion. They speculate that the non-capitalist cultures that are found in indigenous communities may provide a vital space from which new campaigns of resistance can arise.

The book then shifts from analyzing dynamics at the international level, to a closer examination of specific movements within the United States. In his chapter "From Anti-Sweatshop, to Global Justice, to Anti-War: Student Participation in Globalization Protests," Robert Ross compares dynamics in two campus-based organizations. In his analysis, Ross demonstrates that college students have long played key roles in campaigns for social justice, and that they continue to do so today as part of the anti-corporate globalization movement. Kenneth Gould, J. Timmons Roberts, and Tammy Lewis then examine the tenuous alliance that exists between blue-collar workers and the environmentalist green movements. Their chapter, "Blue-Green Coalitions: Constraints and Possibilities in the Post 9/11 Political Environment," describes the optimism that emerged in Seattle in 1999 as workers and environmentalists demonstrated together. But they also highlight points of contention that have re-emerged since then. They conclude by suggesting possibilities for strengthening the blue-green coalition in the coming years. Frederick

Buttel and Kenneth Gould continue this line of analysis, by exploring the possibilities of strengthening cooperation between the anti-corporate and environmental wings of the movement in their chapter "Global Social Movements at the Crossroads."

The concluding chapter by Thomas Reifer, entitled "Torture, Human Rights and the Challenges Facing the Global Peace and Justice Movement," continues this analysis of the new political and security climate that has emerged since September 11, 2001. He argues that the emergence of threats from networks like Al Qaeda has provided an opportunity for US elites to launch an ambitious program of military expansion, which has led to violations of the Geneva conventions and the U.N. Convention Against Torture. Reifer concludes by arguing that activists must resist these troubling developments by increasing their cooperation on an international scale, in spaces like the World Social Forum and at meetings of the Global Anti-War Assembly.

The chapters in this volume are intended to improve our understanding of the opportunities and challenges that surround the anti-corporate globalization movement. Rather than offer uncritically enthusiastic analyses, each of the contributers engages in a nuanced review of the achievements and limitations of the constituent components of this movement. By offering clear-headed analyses, it is hoped that these studies can contribute to the effort to build a vibrant movement that is capable of advocating for ecological sustainability, social justice, and peace on a global level.

Jeffrey M. Ayres

From "Anti-Globalization" to the Global Justice Movement: Framing Collective Action Against Neoliberalism

Introduction

The rise of the so-called "anti-globalization movement" represents one of the most significant illustrations of social conflict and contentious political behavior of the past several decades. The numerous boisterous and well-attended protest events against neoliberal globalization at the turn of the century, moreover, seemed to provide evidence of the rise of an incipient transnational movement. From Seattle, to Chiang Mai, to Prague, to Quebec City and Genoa, domestic and internationally-represented protests developed solidarities, stirred public debate and attracted larger crowds committed to challenging neoliberal policies and institutions. The transnational character of this movement attracted particular attention, and its emergence coincided with a remarkable and increasingly well-documented upsurge in transnational civic activity around a host of global issues, while sparking a mini-publishing industry of "how-to" manuals for budding street activists.[1]

One means of understanding the recent trajectory of this protest movement is to appreciate that its dynamics have been shaped by an underlying and

---

[1] Smith, Pagnucco and Chatfield (1997); Tarrow (2001); Khagram, Riker and Sikkink (2002); Smith and Johnston (2002); Welton and Wolf (2001); Prokosch and Raymond (2002).

quite ferocious contest over people's interpretations and understandings of the supposed benefits of neoliberal economic policies. How people interpret and frame understandings of current economic globalization processes – and how these conceptual framings coalesce to structure global protest – is a process at least as important as how political-economic changes associated with globalization have provoked collective action. In fact, part of the framing contest surrounding the globalization debate has centered on the label "anti-globalization." What we have really been witnessing over the past several years is a maturing of a protest movement against contemporary neoliberal globalization processes. Moreover, critical to this contentious mobilization has been the crystallization of a broadly interpretive, increasingly transnationally-shared diagnostic frame that attributes a variety of social ills to the past 15–20 year span of neoliberal ascendancy.

That the world's economy has been undergoing a neoliberal transformation over the past twenty years is hardly in dispute. Responding to the global economic slowdown as well as increased international competitiveness for markets, which characterized the 1970s, political and business leaders in several key Northern developed states undertook dramatic political-economic reforms designed to channel the globalization of the world's economy in a so-called neoliberal direction. Proponents of neoliberalism, perhaps most notably the Reagan and Thatcher governments of the 1980s, thus pushed for more liberalized trade and investment, tax cuts and concurrent cuts in public spending on social services, deregulation and the privatization of state-owned industries or services. Notably, such a policy direction was at odds with the initial legitimizing basis for the post-World War Two Bretton Woods international economic management system, in which government regulation, social welfare systems and full employment policies were considered an acceptable compliment to essentially still market-based fundamentals.

However, the break with the Bretton Woods regime in the 1970s and the resulting neoliberal turn in the global economy played an important role in shaping the incidences of national, regional and at times apparently transnational protest, which erupted in the 1990s to challenge the neoliberal globalization paradigm. Rising criticism and mounting public demonstrations directed at neoliberal policies and institutions had been occurring globally for some time, but gained particular attention after the 1999 World Trade Organization (WTO) protests in Seattle, raising the specter of a budding legitimacy crisis within the neoliberal paradigm (Useem 2002). Proponents of neoliberal policies insisted that there remained few alternatives to neoliberal globalization, while the protestors asserted that the globalization of the world's economy in fact need not inevitably follow a neoliberal template. Rather, many varied proposals for what was argued to be a more socially, economically and ecologically equitable globalization process began to emerge and to be debated.[2]

This chapter examines the importance of the mobilization of contentious beliefs and interpretations critical of neoliberal globalization. The record of neoliberalism has given activists a wealth of shared experiences from which to fashion a meaningful and increasingly transnationally-shared understanding of the perceived negative effects of such policies. The discussion here focuses broadly on the challenges facing activist civic groups as they have tried to fashion and sustain such a transnational consensus that both attributes blame and develops strategies of action against neoliberal policy initiatives.

The events of September 11, 2001 have clearly muddied the potential trajectory of this protest movement. While some activists have maintained that the mobilization potential of the movement has been little changed by the fallout from the terrorist attacks on the United States, others in the media and various political establishments have been quick to write off the movement's potential. Clearly, the protest movement after September 11 has evolved within a more constrained political environment, with activists facing a markedly resilient state, and a resurgent neoliberal agenda (Ayres and Tarrow 2002). At the same time, the events of September 11 and its aftermath have had an unintended effect of illustrating the durable character of the protest movement, which has surprisingly wide geographic reach.

Collective Action Frames Against Neoliberal Globalization

The concept of framing processes is analytically useful for highlighting how the development and spread of mobilizing ideas is integral to social movement dynamics.[3] For movement activists, framing is "meaning work": an active and contentious process where actors are engaged in producing and disseminating meanings that differ from and may in fact challenge existing

---

[2] For just a few examples see Clark (2003) and Henderson (1999).
[3] Snow et al. (1986); Snow and Benford (1988); Snow and Benford (1992); Benford and Snow (2000).

socio-political conditions. As such, when movement participants "frame" a particular social condition, "they frame, or assign meaning to and interpret events and conditions in ways that are intended to mobilize potential adherents and constituencies, to garner bystander support and to demobilize antagonists" (Snow and Benford 1988: 198). Framing processes thus will be seen to provide a useful conceptual guide for understanding the ongoing struggle to produce and disseminate mobilizing ideas critical of neoliberal globalization.

So-called collective action frames result from this meaning production and serve several crucial functions for movements. Collective action frames are "constructed as movement adherents negotiate a shared understanding of some problematic condition or situation they define as in need of change, make attributions regarding who or what to blame, articulate an alternative set of arrangements and urge others to act in concert to affect change" (Benford and Snow 2000: 613). In other words, collective action frames provide diagnostic attribution, which is concerned with problem identification, and prognostic attribution, which is concerned with problem resolution.

So-called "master frames" serve similar functions to movement specific collective action frames. However, master frames provide broader interpretive paradigms for multiple movements, shaping the outlook of activists and movements. When faced with what are interpreted as unjust social conditions, activists, then, develop movement specific, and sometimes master collective action frames, to highlight the unjust character of events or conditions which are no longer tolerable and are now framed as undefendable. Such frames then provide "legitimizing accounts" shaping and sustaining mobilization campaigns.[4]

Diagnostic Framing: Identifying Neoliberalism as "the Problem"

By the early-to-mid-1990s, many regions of the world had become settings for contentious political debates and social conflicts between opponents and proponents of neoliberal globalization policies. Across these disparate areas, activists were increasingly linking a variety of social, political and economic problems with some of the major developments in the global political econ-

---

[4] McAdam, McCarthy and Zald (1988: 713).

omy. In particular, activists labeled international institutions and regimes associated with the advancement of neoliberal policies, as those factors responsible for some of the economic dislocations and political conflicts of recent years. Thus a process of diagnostic framing was unfolding serving to motivate individuals through movement specific collective action frames that attacked tenets of neoliberalism.

For example, across Western Europe, the first salvos in what would ultimately evolve into what have become the tens-of-thousands strong European Union (EU) summit protests in recent years emerged with opposition to the European Monetary Union proposals implicit in the Maastricht Treaty. Some states, such as Denmark, outright rejected the treaty, while others witnessed widespread popular upheaval against the accord's perceived mandate for fiscal austerity and social cutbacks. The massive and disruptive French general strike against the then Juppé government's economic proposals in the winter of 1995 was but the most dramatic example of this public discord. More widespread and mainstream concerns about an emerging Maastricht-induced European democratic deficit linked constraints bearing down on the sovereign policy-making capacities of EU-member governments, and fed growing popular perceptions of an aloof clique of European business and political elite more concerned with maximizing continental economic efficiency than with addressing mounting social insecurities such as rising unemployment.[5]

Meanwhile, by 1994, a series of popular campaigns against neoliberal policies had buffeted the North American publics in successive waves, from North to South. In Canada, widespread public opposition to the proposed Canada-US Free Trade Agreement (CUSFTA) coalesced in 1988 into a cross-country anti-free trade movement (Ayres 1998). Canadian social activists and nationalists feared liberalizing trade with the U.S. would result in the exodus of jobs, pressure to harmonize social programs and the loss of cultural identity. The anti-free trade movement that emerged played a highly public and intrusive role in the Canadian federal election that autumn, which turned into a de facto referendum on the proposed accord. Despite the eventual ratification of the CUSFTA, the Canadian cross-country coalition-building campaign provided a useful model for U.S. and Mexican groups to adopt in the subse-

---

[5] Geyer and Ayres (1995); Rodrik (1997); Habermas (2001); Ancelovici (2002).

quent campaign against the North American Free Trade Agreement (NAFTA).

Anti-NAFTA mobilizing drew from both national-level campaigns as well as trilateral strategizing and protest actions mounted between Canadian, U.S. and Mexican civil society groups. More specifically, while national groups may have had different mobilization agendas, there was an emergent trilateral collective action frame rooted in a distrust of NAFTA as a thinly veiled neoliberal document. Nationally, innovative new coalitions emerged, such as the Alliance for Responsible Trade (ART) and the Citizens Trade Campaign (CTC) in the U.S., and the Mexican Action Network on Free Trade (RMALC) in Mexico, the latter notably modeling itself after the Canadian anti-free trade coalition. NAFTA's eventual ratification, despite persistent public doubts and civic organizing, ultimately would not be the end of popular discontent. The Zapatista guerrilla movement in the southern Mexican state of Chiapas, began its uprising on behalf of the majority poor indigenous people of Chiapas on January 1, 1994, specifically targeting NAFTA and its neoliberal economic prescriptions for continentally liberalized trade and investment.

Meanwhile, state actors and civil society organizations across the developing South had been mounting their own protests for years against the social fallout caused by IMF structural adjustment programs, the repressive policies of brutal dictatorships or the generalized inequities of the post-World War Two Bretton Woods system. Specifically, the oil shocks of the 1970s and the emergence of the debt crisis in the early 1980s largely shifted the locus of resistance in the developing South to civil society actors. As numerous states across Africa, Latin America and Asia sought to stave off fiscal insolvency, structural adjustment programs were arranged with the International Monetary Fund (IMF), the negative repercussions of which almost always fell on the more vulnerable social actors. In exchange for desperately needed loans, the IMF prescribed deep budget cuts to social spending, a lowering of taxes, increases in interest rates and a general liberalization of trade and investment policies to encourage states across the South to become more hospitable to the arrival of multinational corporations and capital. Frequently lacking institutional allies within the affected polities or organizational resources, including independent labor unions, social actors often responded to these austerity programs with much less organized acts of resistance and protest, including food riots, strikes and other sometimes violent urban street actions. Those groups that did mount better organized grassroots responses to this so-called "shock therapy" also found themselves harassed if not shut down by the military dictatorships and authoritarian regimes which were frequently on the receiving end of IMF loans.[6]

Thus, by the mid-1990s, a number of regional protest campaigns were being shaped by collective actions frames that implicated neoliberal policies and institutions for the mounting inequalities and dislocations of the post-Bretton Woods era. In fact, the record of neoliberalism around the world was less than auspicious and made it easier for activists to assign blame: the total external debt of developing countries had skyrocketed, the gap between the richest and poorest states had grown demonstrably, poverty had increased in many developing states, and the average per capita income growth rate was significantly lower across the developing south than had been the case in the roughly twenty years before the onset of the debt crisis and the policy generalization of the neoliberal model.[7] Furthermore, the international economy had become increasingly unstable, buffeted by a number of financial shocks encouraged by unregulated capital flows. These shocks in Mexico, and then eventually East-Asia, Russia and Brazil, which had evolved out of a globally deregulated market for currency speculation, would further blemish the neoliberal record. Even across portions of the developed North, especially in Western Europe, rising unemployment and the image of increasingly financially straightjacketed welfare systems provoked more widespread public unrest.

In conjunction with this at best uneven neoliberal record, an expanding array of international agreements, which codified neoliberal principles to promote and safeguard liberalized trade and investment, encouraged new expressions of social discontent. NAFTA, the EU Maastricht Treaty, and perhaps most notably, the creation of the WTO in 1995, raised concerns about the hierarchical and elitist structure of trade negotiations and institutions. Moreover, the WTO's new agenda also attracted concern, as in an effort to enforce a rules-based trading system, the institution turned its attention beyond such traditional protectionist devices as tariffs and quotas to a much broader and increasingly controversial array of state laws and regulations that could poten-

---

[6] Acuna and Williams (1994); Walton and Seddon (1994).
[7] Evidence abounds of the uneven results of neoliberal globalization over the past two decades. These examples are drawn from the United Nations (1999) and the World Bank (2000). Also see Weller, Scott and Hersch (2001) and Stiglitz (2002).

tially now be interpreted as trade restrictive. Finally, in light of the WTO's new expanded mandate, attention focused on the lack of international safeguards for labor and human rights, environmental protection and other social concerns.

Towards the Coalescing of a Master Frame Against Neoliberalism

As these disparate collective action frames were shaping regional protests, several important trends were also working to more thoroughly discredit neoliberal policies and institutions, while at the same time legitimate a more widely shared critique of neoliberalism. As the neoliberal record received more widespread and vocal criticism, more space had opened up for civic networking, collective bargaining and political lobbying across a number of developing states, especially across Latin America and South-East Asia, where many states had made transitions to electoral democracies over the previous decade.

At the same time, national civil society organizations from developing states were increasingly networking transnationally with organizations from the developed North at so-called countersummits as well as through the Internet. In particular, so-called "People's Summits," became venues for social activists to meet to share experiences, workshop, strategize and align their national diagnostic frames against the perceived inequities of neoliberal policies and institutions (Korzeniewicz and Smith 2001). These summits, and the increased availability of the Internet, set the stage for the crystallization of an increasingly transnationally-shared diagnostic master frame against neoliberalism.

People's Summits were held parallel to trade minister and heads-of-state gatherings negotiating the proposed Free Trade Area of the Americas (FTAA) in Chile, Brazil and Costa Rica. Similar-style summits were being held to counter the Asia Pacific Economic and Cooperation Forums (APEC) in Vancouver and Manila. One of the more notable counter gatherings took place in Paris in 1997 to strategize and share national perspectives on the proposed Multilateral Agreement on Investment (MAI). The anti-MAI strategy meetings attended by a coterie of civil society organizations helped to spearhead subsequent domestic and international campaigns against the MAI. The MAI negotiations ultimately collapsed when France pulled out, and credited its decision in part to what it referred to as a "global civil society" of anti-MAI activists (Smith and Smythe 1999).

The explosive use of the Internet by thousands of non-governmental organizations would also in fact serve as a key means of bridging a variety of national and regional anti-neoliberal collective action frames. Through the use of listservs, email and web sites, international NGOs as varied as the International Forum on Globalization, the Third World Network, the Hemispheric Social Alliance and the Focus on the Global South, shared information and developed similar critiques of neoliberalism. Hundreds of more nationally-focused NGOs, which were either members of or linked to such larger international organizations, also shared information and critical perspectives gleaned from the Internet in more face-to-face grassroots settings. Hemispheric civil society groups crafted the *Alternatives for the Americas* text,[8] a social-democratic and sustainable-developmental alternative to the proposed FTAA, during parallel People's Summits to the FTAA negotiations, and subsequently edited and revised it via Hemispheric Social Alliance-member Internet exchange.

Opponents of neoliberalism were also energized by U.S. Congressional opposition to the renewal of fast-trade authority. Fast-track power authorizes the U.S. President to negotiate trade accords with foreign countries, with Congress relegated to a reduced role of simply approving or rejecting the proposed accord. With every president since Richard Nixon in the 1970s enjoying this privilege, U.S. President Clinton sought congressional renewal in 1997. However, Clinton withdrew the request in the face of a groundswell of opposition from both labor unions upset with his strong-arming of NAFTA through Congress in 1993, as well as opposition from grassroots lobbying efforts from the CTC and ART coalitions. The following year a reintroduced fast-track proposal went down to defeat, marking a significant trade policy victory for the growing number of civil society organizations across the U.S. who had shown increased skepticism of the supposed benefits of neoliberalism. The Clinton Administration's efforts to reframe the debate over fast-track, by renaming it "trade promotion authority," thereby putting a more benign spin to what was otherwise a tool to promote neoliberal policy proposals, had failed to win reauthorization.

In short, as the 1990s came to a close, a master diagnostic frame critical of neoliberal globalization had slowly crystallized and gained a wider international acceptance. It was not a completely hegemonic counter frame – regional and

---

[8] To read the *Alternatives for the Americas* document, or to retrieve information on the Hemispheric Social Alliance, see http://web.net/comfront.

national-level variations persisted. Yet, the strength of this anti-neoliberal master frame lay in its breadth and capacity to absorb and accommodate the variety of movement and region specific frames that had spurred collective action against neoliberal agreements and institutions over the previous several years. In fact, this master frame had clearly taken on a sufficiently broad interpretive scope in its inclusiveness, cultural reach and flexibility arguably to function as a master "injustice frame" that indicted neoliberalism for a variety of perceived injustices: from environmental degradation, the shifting of jobs to low wages production sites, human rights abuses in sweatshops, and still growing poverty and persistent indebtedness across the developing world.[9] Thus, on the eve of the autumn 1999 protests against the WTO millennial round in Seattle, the parameters of a more clearly transnational diagnostic master collective action frame that would help guide for nearly two years a burgeoning array of large and geographically-varied anti-neoliberal protests had come into focus.

Framing Mobilizations from Seattle to Genoa

The WTO protests in Seattle certainly did not initiate organizing against neoliberalism, but because the protests took place in the United States, they represented an important milestone in such efforts. The tens of thousands strong protests, which disrupted the Seattle WTO meetings, and contributed to the failure by WTO bureaucrats to establish a negotiating agenda, sent a signal of widening discontent both outside and within the U.S. over its official policy embrace of neoliberal principles. Moreover, the image of failure emanating out of Seattle raised some of the most significant questions to that date about the legitimacy of neoliberal policies.

These Seattle protests had been highly visible, drawing upon on eclectic repertoire of tactics: weeks of strategic Internet usage had prepared activists with intimate knowledge of Seattle's downtown layout and WTO delegate's schedules; cellphones aided activists as they spread out across the city engaging in traffic blockading affinity groups; black bloc anarchists resorted to property damage to highly visible corporate symbols of neoliberal success, such as Nike and Starbucks; while thousands of people participated in union rallies and marches (Smith 2001).

---

[9] Klandermans et al. (1999); Benford and Snow (2000).

Moreover, Seattle brought together a collection of diverse, albeit largely U.S.-based groups, whose protests were buttressed by the highly visible and now transnational master collective action frame against neoliberalism. Protestors decried the hierarchical, elitist and closed-door character of the WTO negotiations, and argued that WTO decisions aided and abetted "corporate rule" over popular sovereignty, and facilitated a global "race to the bottom," where corporations exploited conditions of liberalized trade and investment by constantly relocating production to areas with low wage costs and limited government enforcement of social or environmental regulations. There are a number of examples of what could be considered attempts at both diagnostic and prognostic frame alignment processes in books activists produced and disseminated after Seattle.[10] Beyond such books, Internet web sites, activist listservs and the Independent Media Center outlets established throughout the world after Seattle served crucial frame dissemination roles. These activist activities thus challenged the inevitability thesis of neoliberal globalization, stirred what would become a more widespread public debate about the supposed benefits of neoliberal globalization, and put business and political elites on the sudden unexpected defensive against a newly aggressive master frame that challenged the underlying precepts of neoliberalism.

After Seattle, the contest over what "globalization meant" – between the struggle to convince a wider set of domestic and international audiences of the supposed benefits or downsides of neoliberalism – grew intense. This is understandable, as the political context for framing processes frequently changes dramatically between early and more mature periods of collective action, especially after a "movement has established itself as a serious force for social change" (McAdam, McCarthy and Zald 1988: 17). Moreover, framing processes in a maturing movement are the "subject of intense contestation between collective actors representing the movement, the state, and any existing coutermovements" (Ibid.: 16). That political and business elites around the world would react much differently to the anti-neoliberal protest movement following Seattle was then unsurprising.

In fact, a microcosm of the hotly contested framing debate emerged in the middle of the Seattle protests on the opinion pages of the *New York Times*. Following the first and most disruptive day of Seattle protests, *Times'* columnist Thomas Friedman wrote an essay entitled, "Senseless in Seattle," in which

---

[10] Danaher and Burbach (2000); Starr (2000); and Barlow and Clarke (2001).

he decried the WTO protestors as "a Noah's ark of flat-earth advocates, protectionist trade unions and yuppies looking for their 1960s fix" (Freidman 1999). Friedman, an ardent believer in the benefits, if not the inevitability of neoliberal globalization, in effect repudiated the protestors' diagnostic collective action frame.[11] He also contributed to what would become a major plank in the counter-response by supporters of neoliberalism, by labeling protestors as "anti-globalization."

Naomi Klein, Canadian author of *No Logo*, characterized as a "bible" for activists mobilizing against neoliberalism, met Friedman's charges the following day in her own *Times'* essay, entitled, "Rebels in Search of Rules" (Klein 1999). In it Klein refuted Freidman's critique, reiterating the concerns protestors had with neoliberal globalization, and pointedly contesting the "anti-globalization" label. Protestors in Seattle were not against the globalization of economies, cultures and technologies, Klein argued, but against the current WTO-dominated rules-based system that focused mostly on promoting trade and investment liberalization, while remaining silent on consumer, labor, environmental or human rights concerns. What the protestors wanted, Klein argued, were rules for a global economic system that would consider such concerns, and a new global institution that matched a focus for economic growth with considerations of the social and environmental consequences of trade and investment promotion. Interestingly, Klein was rearticulating the contours of the diagnostic frame against neoliberalism, while searching out possible parameters for a prognostic frame.

In fact, while the anti-neoliberal "injustice frame" had performed reasonably well in crafting a transnationally shared diagnosis of neoliberalism's faults, movement activists were having more difficulty undertaking prognostic framing. That is, proposing and agreeing upon plans for attacking neoliberal policies and institutions, as well as in encouraging new movement recruits to literally take to the streets to oppose neoliberal policies, was proving to be a far more difficult task. For, out of Seattle emerged a variety of visions for challenging neoliberalism and for presenting an alternative model to neoliberal globalization.

While some groups sought to "deratify" the existing neoliberal trade and investment arrangements, others sought to reform the WTO, giving it the

---

[11] See *The Lexus and the Olive Tree* (Friedman 2000) for additional details on his analysis.

mandate and enforcement mechanisms to address social and environmental concerns. While some sought to attack and quite literally destroy global capitalism, branding the protest movement "anti-capitalist," others sought a global "New Deal" to create a more social-democratic global system that included such protections as a global minimum wage. Yet, despite these divisions, over the course of the nineteen months from the Seattle protest to the much larger protests in July 2001 against the Group of Eight (G8) Summit in Genoa, Italy, the protest movement mobilized effectively and primarily on the strength of its well-received diagnostic master collective action frame, and was less hobbled by differences at this time over longer-term goals.

After Seattle, increasing numbers of people attended protests, which targeted neoliberal summits and institutions. Notable protest events occurred at: the IMF/World Bank meeting in Washington, DC, April 2000; meetings of the World Economic Forum in Melbourne, Australia, September 2000; IMF/World Bank meetings in Prague, Czech Republic, September 2000; the Asian-Development Bank in Chiang Mai, Thailand, 2000; the 3rd Summit of the Americas FTAA meeting, Quebec City, Canada, April 2001; and the G8 summit, Genoa, Italy, July 2001. Notably, these large summit gatherings did not take place in a vacuum, but were accompanied by numerous parallel national protests across developed and developing states. However, the larger gatherings, especially the summit protests, alternative People's Summits, and the first World Social Forum, which met in Porto Allegre, Brazil in Winter 2001, served as critical diagnostic frame dissemination sites, publicizing, reinforcing and spreading transnationally tenets of the anti-neoliberal collective action frame. Frame alignment processes have been found to be most successful in collective settings (McAdam, McCarthy and Zald 1988), where ideas and sentiments are shared and interpreted. And the proliferation of teach-ins, countersummits, street theater and dramaturgy proved crucial in transnationalizing the anti-neoliberal diagnostic frame.

On the eve of the Genoa, Italy G8 protest, then, politicians, business leaders and media outlets were paying increased attention to the concerns of the movement, as the "Washington Consensus" that had sustained the neoliberal globalization frame appeared to be cracking.[12] Suddenly the World Bank was professing an interest in sustainable development projects, international institutions were becoming more open to NGO participation, politicians were

---

[12] Broad and Cavanaugh (1999); Useem (2001).

entertaining thoughts of much more dramatic debt relief for impoverished states as well as taxes on global currency speculation, while debates over neoliberalism became much more common editorial page fare.

At the same time, the anti-neoliberal protest movement appeared to have gained momentum, propelled by an eclectic set of protest repertoires combined with a general transnational consensus between civil society groups against the abuses of corporate power and corporate influence over popular democratic decision-making processes. Civil society groups and activists shared a strong sense of what they felt was "wrong" with neoliberalism; what remained unresolved was the development of collectively shared and agreed upon solutions and strategic responses to these problems.

After September 11: The Altered Terrain for Anti-Neoliberal Protest

The terrorist attacks on the United States on September 11, 2001 had a dramatic and immediate effect on the mobilization potential for activism against neoliberal institutions. The fallout from the attacks exposed weaknesses in the anti-neoliberal collective frame, temporarily dampened enthusiasm, at least in the U.S., for large-scale contentious protest, and illustrated forcefully the continued relevance of the state in the structuring of movement activity. Over time, moreover, the limits especially of prognostic framing processes would also become apparent as activists would struggle to develop coherent plans of action for challenging neoliberal policies and institutions. Figure 1 illustrates both the framing contest that had ensued, especially following the Seattle WTO protests, as well as the differences between interpretive beliefs germane to anti-neoliberal diagnostic and prognostic framing processes.

In fact, state authorities adopted a much more aggressive approach towards containing protests as well as in reasserting a multi-pronged neoliberal agenda. On the one hand, with the passage of such legislation as the USA Patriot Act, it became easier for U.S. government agencies to criminalize dissent – a tactical approach that had begun prior to September 11 – but one that gained greater legitimacy thereafter as authorities publicly equated protests against neoliberal globalization with terrorism.[13] Thus, while protestors still rallied

---

[13] In the immediate aftermath of the terrorist attacks, Italian Prime Minister Sylvio Berlusconi mused on the "singular coincidence" between the terrorist attacks in the U.S. and the protests against neoliberal globalization. Meanwhile, U.S. Trade

Figure 1. Contested Interpretations of Globalization Processes.

Actors	Arguments/Claims	Policy Proposals

anti-neoliberal protest
movement
 	
– civil society activists
– national/transnational
  social movement
  organizations
– Independent Media
  Centers
– Internet web sites
	– race to the bottom
	– democratic deficit
	– hierarchical
	– non-transparent
	– deliberate political process
	– corporate rights
		– deratify
		– reform existing treaties
		– debt relief
		– strengthen state
		  sovereignty
		– deglobalize
		– return to the local

neoliberalism proponents
(countermovement)
 	
– states
– multi-national
  corporations
– currency speculators
– financial media outlets
– IMF/World Bank/WTO
	– there is no alternative
	– inevitable, desirable
	  process
	– irreversable
	– best prescription for
	  economic growth
		– liberalized trade and
		  investment
		– deregulate
		– cut taxes
		– privatize
		– reduce public
		  expenditures

at the New York City meeting of the World Economic Forum in January 2002, the police presence was so extensive, and the aftershocks of September 11 still so fresh, that both the opportunities and the appetite for large contentious protests was missing.

This pattern of maintaining a large police presence continued to thwart large-scale demonstrations, especially across North America. From the meeting of the Group of 8 leading industrialized states in Kanaskas, Alberta in summer 2002, to the following July WTO ministerial meeting in Montreal, Quebec, police curtailed demonstrations and kept activists off-balance with preemptive arrests and security perimeters (Thanh Ha 2003).

Representative Robert Zoellick in a speech in Washington D.C. hinted at what he felt were "intellectual connections" between terrorists and "others who have turned to violence to attack international finance, globalization and the United States." See Erlanger (2001); Palast (2001); Stewart (2001); Scher (2001); Della Porta and Tarrow (2002); Panitch (2002).

It was clear, moreover, that U.S. activists were on the defensive and hesitant about their tactical direction after September 11, as large-scale raucous protests seemed out of step with the national mood.[14] The state responses to both the terrorist attacks as well as to anti-neoliberal protest, posed a challenge to prognostic frame dissemination, as activists now had to engage in a public relations battle to de-link in the minds of an anxious U.S. public, protest against neoliberal policy from acts of terrorism. Moreover, growing anti-war activism – first as the U.S. invaded Afghanistan to overthrow the Taliban regime, and then once the Bush Administration quickly refocused for a possible war with Iraq – posed a challenge to sustaining an anti-neoliberal collective action frame. The energy devoted to straightening out the protest movement's identity and the meaning behind any new demonstrations was draining, as many protest groups struggled to reconcile being both opposed to neoliberal globalization and pro-peace (Huber and McCallum 2002).

At the same time, as activists across the U.S. worked to clarify their post-September 11 strategies for challenging neoliberalism, the Bush Administration embarked on a campaign to strategically reassert the neoliberal agenda. Only weeks after the terrorist attacks, President Bush told business leaders at the Shanghai meeting of the APEC forum, that terrorism could be defeated through the promotion of free trade, while U.S. Federal Reserve Chairman Greenspan argued that the attacks on the U.S. made it even more urgent that the WTO talks in Qatar succeed (Wayne 2001). The renewal of fast-track trade negotiating authority became a test of patriotism for waffling members of Congress (Sanger 2001), and by July 2002, Bush had won reauthorization of this power. Once equipped with this negotiating tool, the Bush administration would focus on aggressively advancing neoliberal policy goals through parallel tracks in the ongoing FTAA hemispheric discussions, as well as within the Doha, Qatar round.[15]

Beyond the challenges faced by activists in the U.S., regional and tactical differences within the protest movement against neoliberalism became much more apparent. Clearly, civil society groups during the late 1990s had found it increasingly easier to develop shared and ultimately transnational under-

---

[14] See for example Carter and Barringer (2001); Wayne (2001); and Fries (2002).

[15] Despite marginalizing protestors from the FTAA and WTO negotiating sessions, policy divisions especially between developing and developed states over agricultural subsidies in the developed North, increasingly threaten to derail both the regional and global neoliberal trade agenda. See Drohan (2003).

standings of the experiences and problems fostered on different regions by neoliberal economic policies, than in devising mutually reconcilable strategic responses to these problems (Stuart 2003). Differences of opinion, illustrative of the limits of anti-neoliberal prognostic framing, starkly emerged in setting such as the World Social Forum, over a variety of tactics and goals.[16] Questions that confronted activists included: what are the more effective tactics for challenging neoliberal policies: more consultative and collaborative engagement in neoliberal summitry by NGOs, or grassroots mobilization and contentious protest?[17] Moreover, what are the appropriate and mutually acceptable goals for the movement: to reform the existing global capitalist system, or to deratify existing trade agreements? Should activists work to strengthen state sovereignty or move beyond the state to "return to the local" in the pursuit of "deglobalization?"[18]

The persistent North-South divide, in terms of resource availability, organizational strength, and the underlying technological digital divide, also challenged differently the capacity of regional civil society groups to continue to connect local grassroots concerns to transnational protest campaigns. Such resource asymmetries have become recently apparent, for example, in the hemispheric mobilization against the FTAA. Civil society group divisions over tactics and resources have challenged the legitimacy of the Hemispheric Social Alliance as a broadly-based transnational social movement organization, and revealed strategic splits between groups desiring an insider role in summit deliberations versus those groups who view themselves as outsiders and supportive of large-scale civil disobedience against FTAA neoliberal summitry.[19]

Conclusion

The mobilization of beliefs and interpretations critical of neoliberal globalization has been central to the eruption of a protest movement that has achieved global proportions. Movement and region-specific collective action

---

[16] Cooper (2002); Faux (2003).
[17] To sample such discussions see Klein (2001), Grundy and Howell (2001), and Penniman (2002).
[18] For discussions of the different possible goals for the anti-neoliberal movement, see Narsalay (2002); Scholte (2002); Bello (2002); Laxer (2003).
[19] Korzeniewicz and Smith (2001); Smith (2002); Massicotte (2003).

frames critical of the impact of neoliberal policy were shaped out of contentious struggles that preceded by well over a decade the eventual development of protests of larger scale and global scope. A master collective action frame rooted in a diagnosis of neoliberalism's policy ills served as a broadly inclusive interpretative medium, targeting for blame neoliberal policies such as unfettered trade and investment and the rulings of institutions such as the WTO and the IMF.

However, it was the very inclusiveness and accommodating character of this anti-neoliberal master frame – embracing in its diagnosis such varied concerns as the degradation of the environment, emerging democratic deficits and the decline of popular sovereignty, human rights abuses under sweatshop conditions, or even opposition to the U.S. war with Iraq or the rights of Palestinian refugees – which limited prognostic framing processes, exposing divisions within the international community of activists over proposed strategies for carrying out plans of action against neoliberalism.

Yet, despite the more challenging environment for prognostic framing, the fallout from the terrorist attacks on the United States has had an unanticipated effect: it has served to illustrate the durable character of the protest movement against neoliberalism. That is, the movement has evolved and prospered despite the constraints bearing down particularly on U.S. activists. Events since September 11 refute those claims by critics asserting that the movement was largely comprised of labor union protectionists from wealthy Northern states. Rather, the most significant and innovative protest events have continued outside North America. A transnational diagnostic frame critical of neoliberalism has remained a durable feature of demonstrations against neoliberal policies after September 11, even if these protests have retained a national or regional flavor dependent especially on the availability of activists and SMOs most closely at hand.

For example, the World Social Forum initially held annually in Porto Alegre, Brazil, and then in 2004 in Mumbai, India, continues to draw greater numbers of people and represents a crucial forum for potentially developing a more widely accepted prognostic frame against neoliberalism. Moreover, the parallel regional social forums, which have sprouted up independent of, but nonetheless inspired by, the annual WSF, illustrate that various regional civil society groups remain receptive to the overarching anti-neoliberal collective action frame. The European Social Forum held in Florence, Italy in November 2002, drew over one million people, the Asian Social Forum held in Hyderabad,

India in January 2003 attracted 15,000 activists, while organizers across North America organized a series of social forums in select cities throughout 2003 and 2004. These regional social forums are rooted in the experiences of national civil society group opposition to neoliberal policy, but are tied together in the larger transnational diagnostic collective action frame that continues to express itself out of Porto Alegre with the slogan, "Another World Is Possible" (Bidwai 2003).

There continues to be as well numerous examples of regional and transnationally-coordinated contentious protests against neoliberal policy initiatives. Hundreds of protest events took place in cities around the world to coincide with the 4th Ministerial meeting of the WTO in Doha, Qatar in November 2001. Regionally, anti-FTAA protests occurred in Quito, Ecuador in autumn 2002, against the 7th Ministerial Meeting of the FTAA. These protests were backed by a variety of North and South American solidarity events, with the Quito protests specifically benefiting from North-South civil society collaboration (Ruben 2002). In fact, prognostic hemispheric frame alignment against the FTAA seems to be increasingly rooted in a growing option for the use of more combative tactics, indicative of the degree of opposition that exists across this region to the possible implementation of a hemispheric neoliberal agreement.

Finally, it is clear that in the midst of this continued transnational activism, the state has not lost the capacity to control events within its boundaries, and it will continue to play an important role in structuring protest. The current economic crisis affecting Latin America, captured in the Argentine meltdown and the rejection of neoliberal policy prescriptions by the tens-of-millions who elected the Brazilian Workers Party candidate, Luis Inacio Lula da Silva into the president's office, suggests that critically positioned states in the world economy may become vocal opponents of the expansion of neoliberal policy, with Brazil potentially the leading roadblock to the successful completion of FTAA negotiations. In short, the protest movement against neoliberalism may gain new momentum from states, which ultimately retain the greatest capacity to influence and reform those political processes that have produced over two decades of hotly contested neoliberal policy initiatives. Any success in developing widely shared prognostic frames against neoliberalism may in turn depend upon the concerted opposition of centrally placed states who may share with activist civil society organizations innovative ideas for reforming current neoliberal arrangements.

Jackie Smith

Exploring Connections Between Global Integration and Political Mobilization[1]

Introduction

Although many Americans were surprised by the size and vigor of the recent protests against the global trade regime, these events should be seen as part of a long and growing stream of protest against global financial institutions. This resistance has been most visible in the global South, where the effects of global financial policies have triggered the most violent responses. The protests have broadened geographically and gained momentum since the late 1970s.[2] The most recent protests are especially important in that they demonstrate strong opposition to global trade liberalization from a variety of constituencies within the countries that have benefited the most from liberal trade policies. They also build upon a more extensive network of transnational organiza-

[1] This is a revised version of paper presented at the American Sociological Association Annual Meeting, Anaheim, CA, 18 August 2001. This research has been supported by an American Sociological Association-National Science Foundation Funds for Advancing the Discipline grant, and by the World Society Foundation. Numerous colleagues provided helpful comments on various aspects of this research, including my colleagues in the sociology department and in the social movements discussion group at SUNY Stony Brook, members of the Labor and Globalization seminar at Columbia University, the Globalization study group at the University of Pittsburgh, the Globalization and Contentious Politics seminar at Cornell University, and students and faculty at the Sociology/Anthropology department at Hofstra University. Special thanks to Dawn Wiest for research assistance on the project and to John McCarthy, Timothy Moran, Sidney Tarrow, Kiyoteru Tsutsui, and Andrea Tyree for comments on earlier drafts.
[2] Cf. Keck (1998); Fox and Brown (1998); Walton and Seddon (1994).

tional and informational ties among activists in a wide range of countries. This organizational infrastructure began to expand in the latter half of the 20th century, and its roots took hold and generated more rapid transnational organizational expansion in the 1970s and 1980s (Sikkink and Smith 2002).

While the post-September 11 context in the United States has stifled political dissent of all kinds, the terrorist attacks on the World Trade Center did not dampen protests outside the U.S. In fact, they may have enhanced their urgency and swelled their numbers, as more people express fears about the dangers of U.S. unilateralism. The rise of transnationally coordinated terrorism and other, non-violent, forms of resistance grow from the same global processes: both are facilitated by the proliferation of cheap technologies for transnational communication and travel and both benefit from opportunities to cross borders to mobilize supporters and other resources. Both also highlight the failures of prevailing socio-economic institutions to respond to the needs and interests of growing numbers of people. Ultimately, the success of the so-called "war on terror" may depend more upon strengthening those groups that advocate a greater democratization of global institutions – an inherently nonviolent claim – than upon waging a hot war against leaders of militant forms of resistance. A greater understanding the nature of this infrastructure for global social change organizing can help us identify possibilities for cultivating global citizen alliances that can respond to the challenges of globalization.

Global Integration and Social Movement Mobilization

How should we expect global integration to affect social movements? Social movement scholars have recognized various potential transnational impacts on social movement mobilization. First, the relative strength or weakness of a state and its degree of vulnerability to domestic political challengers is affected by the state's geopolitical position. For instance, world-systems theory holds that core states will tend to be more democratic, while periphery states will tend to be more repressive. Thus, the political opportunities that movements in every country face are shaped by how the target government is integrated into the global political economy.[3] Second, the ideas around which social movements mobilize have long flowed freely across political

---

[3] Cf. Maney (2002); Anderson-Sherman and McAdam (1982); Skocpol (1979).

boundaries. Thus, civil rights activists drew inspiration and strategy from Mahatma Gandhi while European and U.S. activists of the 1960s learned from each others' experiences and innovations.[4] More recently, transnational alliances of environmental activists and indigenous groups have generated a "political ecology" frame that relates environmental struggles to concerns for human rights and local empowerment (Rothman and Oliver 2002).

Third, transformations in global communication and transportation technologies as well as the related development of global economic and political institutions facilitate the mobilization of transnationally organized social movements.[5] They do so in part by fostering the development of shared cultural and ideological frameworks that serve to legitimate certain collective values and goals – such as democracy, human rights, or free trade – that appeal to global or at least transnational constituencies.

Not only have social movements been affected by changes in the global political and economic order, but they have also played roles in shaping that order. For instance, Keck and Sikkink (1998) show how advocates working to abolish the slave trade, helped to advance transnational human rights norms. In addition, numerous case studies have documented that the formation and strengthening of intergovernmental organizations (IGOs) such as the United Nations have been assisted by efforts of non-governmental actors to shape governmental policies and to codify universal standards for, among other issues, human rights and more humane military and national defense practices. The recent mobilizations around global trade institutions have built in part upon efforts to defend prior achievements in global environmental, human rights and labor law from growing challenges by the global trade regime.[6]

Rates of change in the quantity and speed of economic, political, and other societal interactions have increased dramatically, particularly in more recent times. Forms of economic globalization can be traced back to the late 17th

---

[4] Kumar (1992); Chabot (2000); McAdam and Rucht (1993).

[5] Keck and Sikkink (1998) discuss the formation of less formally organized transnational "issue networks" promoting changes such as the abolition of the slave trade, an end to foot-binding in China, and expansion of women's suffrage. These issue networks resemble what sociologists call social movements, though there are some important conceptual differences, such as a distinction between governmental agents and actors promoting some form of political change (Smith, Pagnucco and Chatfield 1997). See also Kriesberg (1997); Guidry, Kennedy, and Zald (2000).

[6] Hovey (1997); Smith (1995); Boli and Thomas (1999); Smith (2002a); Evangelista (1995); Finnemore (1996); Price (1998).

century or earlier.[7] Political globalization – first characterized by the diffusion of organizational templates for state structures and political organization, and later evolving towards an increasingly organized inter-state polity – dates back at least as far (Boli and Thomas 1997). Socio-cultural globalization developed from the transnational human interactions manifested in economic and political integration. The technological and organizational innovations, particularly those of the late-20th century, have accelerated capacity for global integration of economic and political activities, and these same innovations have also served to advance globalization of the social and cultural realm.

The changes in all three dimensions of globalization affect the variable political opportunities available to social movement actors (della Porta and Kriesi 1999). The economic realm is characterized by increasing income disparities and concentrations of wealth in the hands of transnational corporate actors coupled with the strengthening – particularly during the 1990s – of international institutions designed to facilitate and advance free trade. These developments have important consequences both for the formation of new grievances and for the capacities of challengers to mobilize and to affect social change.[8] In the political realm, the formation and strengthening of supranational institutions has transferred important aspects of political decision making outside the nation-state. This undermines democratic accountability within states, thereby limiting the abilities of challengers to achieve certain policy goals within national political arenas alone. It has, however, also created new opportunities for social movements and other non-state actors to access decision makers and to seek influence in both national and transnational policy arenas.[9]

Finally, in the socio-cultural realm, the global spread of ideas (e.g., universal human rights) and cultural materials (e.g., films, music) may help lay the organizational and ideological foundations for transnational collective action. It also creates new incentives for contention as social movement actors

---

[7] Wolf (1982); Chase-Dunn and Hall (1997).

[8] Cf. Korzeniewicz and Moran (1997); Sassen (1998).

[9] Cf. Smith, Pagnucco and Chatfield (1997). Japanese environmental organizations gained increased access to national politicians as a direct result of the Climate Change Convention negotiations in Kyoto. The international conference increased the salience of environmental issues on national political agendas, and it legitimated the claims of national environmental groups. Moreover, the United Nations practice of recognizing non-governmental actors socialized Japanese officials to expand the access of Japanese NGOs to national political arenas.

seek to align the framing of local conflicts with those of global-level discourses. By framing local struggles in global terms, local groups can gain legitimacy for their cause as well as new international allies. The various aspects of globalization, in short, affect the political opportunities open to movements at both the national and international levels, the resources available to movement actors, and the interpretations (or framing) of conflicts. Nevertheless, efforts to understand how these global economic, institutional, and social transformations affect possibilities for social movements remain relatively under-developed.[10]

Global Integration and Social Movements

How are changes in international political and economic interactions likely to affect the mobilization of transnational social movements? Boli and Thomas (1997) documented the presence of a "world polity" that is evidenced by isomorphism in the organizational structures adopted by national states as well as by the global diffusion of ideas such as individualism, scientific rationality, bureaucratization, and citizenship. They see international non-governmental organizations (INGOs) as important conveyors of world cultural ideas and values because these groups advocate common international standards for industries or to advance the goals of democracy, human rights, or respect for the environment. Kathryn Sikkink and her colleagues have done important work to demonstrate the ways that certain INGOs advance global norms and shape inter-state politics.[11] This research leads us to expect to find relationships between changes in the broader global political environment and those transnational organizations promoting social change.

The second half of the 20th century has also brought a dramatic expansion of supranational political institutions. Governments have been cooperating around an increasing number of issues – from the rules of war and humanitarian law to environmental practices to the policing of international narcotics trafficking. And they have established formal organizations to structure and routinize this cooperation. This pattern of increased formalization and bureaucratization of inter-state structures parallels that accompanying the

---

[10] Cf. Snow et al. (1986); Tarrow (2001); and Tarrow (forthcoming).
[11] Keck and Sikkink (1998); Risse, Ropp, and Sikkink (1999); Khagram, Riker and Sikkink (2002).

rise of the modern state. Social movement analysts trace the rise of organized social movements to the emergence of national states during the 18th century.[12] We should therefore expect greater formalization within a social movement sector that seeks to influence the political contests being waged in emerging supra-national institutions. In other words, just as the rise of states brought with it the emergence of national social movement organizations (SMOs), we should expect an expansion of IGOs to generate new forms of transnational organization, or transnational SMOs.

Early states altered political contests between challengers and elites by bringing a new actor into what once were more regional and local conflicts. That state brought increasing amounts of resources to bear on those conflicts and served as either opponent or ally of local challengers, depending upon the context. The same dynamic is true when we think of the struggles in a global political context. International agencies are created and funded by national governments. They are charged with addressing specific international *problems*, and they therefore do not always reflect the specific *interests* of their government members. This creates opportunities for cooperation between international agencies and transnational social movement actors around problem-solving goals.[13] Such cooperation between SMOs and IGOs can contribute to movement mobilization as well as co-optation.

Once established, international institutions can stimulate growth in the transnational social movement sector by providing access to information and financial resources, by serving as a focal point or target for social movement energies, and by actively facilitating networking among participants in social movements. The end of the Cold War meant that superpower rivalries no longer stymied negotiations in the United Nations, creating new optimism for multilateralism. It allowed new issues to achieve greater priority on international agendas, and it opened up space for the emergence of new political blocs.

At least at first, this produced new levels of agreement within the UN and generated new treaty initiatives in several issue areas outside of the area of military security. By facilitating cross-national dialogue among actors from

---

[12] Cf. Tilly (1984); Markoff (1996, 1999).

[13] Thus, we see that social movement actors promoting limits to greenhouse gas emissions often find ready allies and resources from governments that favor a stronger climate change treaty (such as the Nordic governments) and from international agencies (such as the Secretariat for the Climate Change Convention). These allies and resources are part of a broader struggle against other states (e.g., the U.S.) and industry (which created its own "NGO" – called the "Global Climate Coalition" – in order to resist stronger environmental accords).

both within and outside governments, by focusing government attention and resources on problems defined through international negotiations, and by conveying legitimacy to some of the claims of social movements, international institutions influence transnational mobilization. We should expect, then, that an increase in the numbers of organizations, conferences, and treaties that help structure international political cooperation will affect the shape of the transnational social movement sector.

Another crucial trend in the post-Cold War period is the expansion of neoliberal ideology, especially through the World Trade Organization and regional trade associations as well as in the policies of the World Bank and IMF. The demise of the Soviet Union was seen as a victory for free market capitalism over socialist economic policies, and proponents of limited government and unrestricted markets enjoyed important influence in the global economic arena. The opening of the World Trade Organization in 1994 clearly affected all multilateral policies, and as the organization took hold, it became clear that its operation could threaten other areas of international cooperation such as human rights and the environment. These developments should be expected to affect the character transnational social movement organizations, probably by attracting greater attention to trade and economic issues.

Economic globalization has important consequences for transnational social movement mobilization; and not least among them is the diffusion of inexpensive communications and transportation technologies that are essential to transnational corporate operations. Does the social movement sector replicate existing structures of economic dominance and marginalization? Are challengers to existing global inequities subject to economic forces that reinforce gaps between the world's rich and poor?

Participation in many transnational political and social change activities demands highly specialized knowledge and skills. At the very least, one is required to speak at least one of the official UN languages. And more ready access to information and officials is available if a TSMO is based near a center of international decision making such as New York, Brussels, or Geneva. Those promoting international human rights must have some expertise in law, and many activists in this area hold advanced degrees in that field. Moreover, the domination of many global institutions by the agendas and interests of core industrialized countries would lead us to expect that the core/periphery pattern might be replicated in the social movement sector. However, the fact that TSMOs are, by definition, challengers to the existing political and economic order, we would expect that they would not simply mirror and reinforce structural inequalities, but rather that they would seek to transform them (Amin et al. 1990). Thus, we would expect core/periphery differences in the social movement sector to be shrinking over time, particularly as the sector itself becomes more organizationally rich and diverse.

An additional area of concern regards the ways that changing technologies – particularly the expansion of electronic communications – affect transnational organizing. We should expect that expanding global integration of social, economic, and political relations both reflects and contributes to new opportunities for transnational organizing of all kinds. Technologies that facilitate transnational communication and routine exchanges of ideas as well as international conferences and exchanges that bring individuals and organizational representatives together help reduce the costs of building and maintaining transnational organizations. They therefore increase the feasibility of individuals' direct participation in transnational organizations, rather than indirect participation through national sections.

At the same time, globalization processes are fraught with uncertainties and rapid change. Anticipating the course of complex inter-state negotiations and the applications of international law poses major challenges for transnational actors, including businesses as well as activists. In order to avoid unforeseen calamities or to take advantage of emerging opportunities, transnational actors must be able to respond quickly. They also must have the capacity to mobilize differently in different parts of the world. Just as businesses must tailor their marketing and industrial strategies to local contexts (see, e.g., Sklair 2001), so, too, must transnational social movement actors cultivate mobilizing strategies that are appropriate to local or regional cultural and strategic conditions. Thus, we would expect to find that transnational movement structures will become more decentralized and informal over the recent decades of expanding global integration.

Methods & Data

Formal organizations provide important infrastructures that aid activists in their efforts to mobilize and act collectively to promote social change. Earlier work suggests that social movement organizations that adopt transnational organizational structures play key roles in mobilizing, informing, and coordinating collective action on issues crossing national boundaries. Thus, this study examines the characteristics of formal transnational organizations advocating social change.

Evidence about changes in the transnational social movement sector come from the *Yearbook of International Associations* (see Appendix for details about the data). Each edition of the *Yearbook* was reviewed to identify free-standing non-governmental associations that were specifically organized to promote some type of social or political change goal. The list includes groups ranging from Amnesty International to the Universal Esperanto League to a few anti-abortion organizations. Development organizations are included in the dataset only if their entry suggests that they advocate for poor empowerment rather than simply provide for the delivery of services.

Below I explore how the transnational social movement sector changed during a period when the international system itself witnessed a dramatic transformation that included more extensive international engagement. I begin to inquire into the assumptions outlined above using data the transnational social movement sector during the 1990s. While additional case study data are needed to fully test the hypotheses, we can begin here to identify patterns and develop lines of future inquiry into the dynamics of transnational organizing.

We anticipated that increasing global integration would both necessitate and create opportunities for transnational mobilization. Given that the end of the Cold War has been accompanied by efforts to expand the agendas and jurisdictions of global political and economic institutions, we should expect to find growth in the numbers of new transnational organizations formed during this period. Also, we would expect that these trends would help already existing groups to mobilize members from more countries.

Although we find dramatic growth in the numbers of TSMOs over recent decades, in comparison to the growth rates of previous decades, Figure 1 shows that substantially fewer new groups were formed during the 1990s than we might expect. While the *rate* of growth in the population was around 100% for the 1970s and 1980s, it was just under 50% for the 1990s. Moreover, the average numbers of new organizations formed in the five years prior to each data collection point declined from an average of 21.8 in 1993 to 17.4 in 2000. We also did not find expansion in the numbers of countries in which TSMOs report members. Although the average number of countries with members increased slightly – from 31.0 to 34.4 – between 1983 and 2000, the median number of countries remains unchanged, despite the increased numbers of states in the post Cold-war era.

The most plausible explanation for this finding is that, as the density of this population increases, competition for resources and members inhibits the formation of new groups.[14] Given a limited pool of resources and the high costs of transnational organizing, activists seeking to take advantages of new international political opportunities may seek more cost-effective ways of doing this than starting a new international organization. Thus, although the 1990s may have expanded the "opportunity structure" in the international system, these changes could not sustain the high rates of organizational growth that we saw in the 1980s. Nor did they encourage existing organizations to expand significantly their geographic scopes. If the 1990s and expanding global integration did indeed provided impetus for more activists to engage in transnational activism, this new activism is not reflected in the formation of new organizations.

It may be that existing organizational structures were able to respond to the more favorable political conditions of the 1990s by expanding to incorporate new members and program agendas. The political environment itself

Transnational Social Movement Organizations

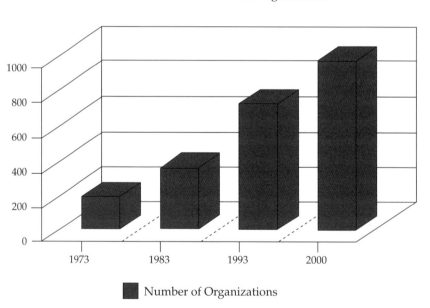

Number of Organizations

Data for 1973 were collected in collaboration with Kathryn Sikkink (see Sikkink and Smith 2002).

---

[14] Cf. Minkoff (1995); Hannan and Freeman (1977).

might also have encouraged this. For instance, the 1992 United Nations Conference on Environment and Development (UNCED) led to an unprecedented move within the UN system to allow *national* and *sub-national* groups to perform tasks that were once the domain of transnational SMOs. Whereas prior to 1992 formal accreditation at the UN required a transnational organizational structure, the UNCED Secretariat allowed national groups to apply for formal accreditation to the conference, and this precedent led to the adoption of similar rules in other UN venues.[15] Before 1992, national groups seeking to work within the UN system needed to develop an affiliation with a transnationally organized group that had official accreditation. However, the UNCED process opened the door for national groups to develop direct contacts with UN offices, reducing the need for nationally based activists to join in formal international alliances in order to target the UN.

During the 1990s, global institutions expanded their scopes and global conferences sponsored by the United Nations encouraged mobilization around particular issues.[16] This is likely to have affected how social movements framed their own struggles. Table 1 displays the issues around which TSMOs organized.

We find here that human rights remains the major issue around which the largest numbers of TSMOs organize, and a consistent quarter of all groups work principally on this issue. The environment has attracted growing attention since the early 1970s. And between 1983 and 2000, development issues motivated a larger percentage of transnational SMOs. This parallels a growing international discourse on development and inequality that intensified with the end of the Cold War. Many analysts characterized the shift from Cold War to Post-Cold War politics as one from East-West to North-South conflict, as negotiations on trade liberalization and development displaced attention to arms control. Most UN Conferences reflected the economic divisions between the global North and South, as many global problems were linked to inequalities and development failures.

---

[15] Formal accreditation at UN Conferences enables organizations to have access to official proceedings, provides access to official documentation surrounding the meeting, and provides limited speaking rights in official, inter-governmental meetings. Immediately following UNCED, national and sub-national groups were granted the rights to participate formally in the annual Commission on Sustainable Development, whose role was to monitor national governments' follow-up to UNCED. Other UN agencies followed this precedent as they re-evaluated their NGO accreditation process.

[16] The UN sponsored an unprecedented number of such conferences during the 1990s on issues ranging from environment and development (1992) to women's rights (1995) to housing (1997) and population (1994).

Table 1. Issue Focus of Transnational Social Movement Organizations
Number of Organizations (Percentage).

	1973 N=183	1983 N=348	1993 N=711	2000 N=959
Human Rights	22%	26%	28%	26%
Environment	9	12	18	17
Peace	12	11	11	10
Women's Rights	9	7	9	9
Development/empowerment	4	4	7	10
Global Justice/Peace/Envir.	4	4	4	11
Self-determination/Ethnic unity	7	7	3	2
Multi-issue organizations*	7%	12%	12%	17%

* This categorization overlaps some of the categories above – especially the global justice category.

A robust trend we see in the 1990s is a shift towards more multi-issue organizing by TSMOs. The number of groups adopting multi-issue organizing frames doubled between 1993 and 2000. Interestingly, groups organized within the global South were significantly more likely to engage in multi-issue organizing.[17] This would suggest that Southern TSMOs face different mobilizing opportunities and constraints from their Northern and trans-regional counterparts. Such differences may arise from more repressive political contexts that may foster frames that approach highly contentious issues such as equity and human rights from angles that may appear less contentious. One such example would be the Greenbelt Movement in Kenya, which originated as a women's tree-planting organization and subsequently expanded its frame to issues such as empowerment and equitable development (Michaelson 1994).

Also, groups in the South often aim to cultivate ties with Northern counterparts in order to bring external financial and symbolic resources for their struggles. This may mean that they must adapt their frames to fit those that resonate with Northern audiences. Most prominent among these kinds of cases are indigenous rights groups that extend or bridge their issue-frames to demonstrate connections between human rights and environmental degra-

---

[17] Twenty-six percent of groups organized in the South indicated a multi-issue organizing frame, compared to 17% of North-only and trans-regional (e.g., both North and South) organizations (p < .05). The North-South differences here are mirrored in two surveys of transnational human rights and environmental organizations.

dation.[18] Another possible explanation is that populations in the South face experiences that make the connections between global economic divisions and other issues much more obvious. Under such conditions, organizing for peace or human rights without explicitly identifying the underlying economic sources of conflict would be ineffective.

Another trend towards greater multi-issue frames is reflected in the growing numbers of groups organizing around a broad global justice/peace/environment frame. This development also parallels expanding multilateral cooperation on trade issues that characterizes the post-Cold War period. Multi-issue groups grew from just 4% in the early 1990s to 11% by 2000. If my earlier interpretation of the causes of more frequent multi-issue organizing in the global South are correct, then the intensification of global economic integration during the 1990s would have helped reproduce the kinds of experiences faced in the global South more broadly – making it easier for even Northern activists to make connections between economic inequalities and other problems.

The issue of ethnic unity/liberation drew declining attention as the organizing focus of TSMOs. The most recent period again saw a decline in the absolute numbers of such TSMOs from 26 to 20. This can signal two very different trends. One is that these types of movements are adopting – probably in response to the elimination of Cold-War induced transfers of military aid – more militant, illicit tactics and therefore are less likely to report their activities in the *Yearbook*. Another possibility is that activists are framing ethnic struggles in new ways in response to changing issue priorities on the international agenda. Rather than advocating separatist goals, for instance, they may seek to mobilize around more inclusive, transnational identities such as indigenous peoples or refugees. Such identities allow groups to take advantage of treaties and other opportunities in international institutions that legitimize individual human rights claims and challenge traditional notions of state sovereignty based on self-determination.[19]

For instance, groups like the Federal Union of European Nationalities or the World Council of Indigenous Peoples may help focus the efforts of multiple different ethnic groups around the aim of using global institutions to protect minority groups' rights against infringements by states and other actors. The data here support this interpretation. About half of the groups

---

[18] Cf. Brysk (1996); Rothman and Oliver (2002).
[19] Brysk (2000); Sassen (1998: 22).

working to promote indigenous peoples' rights were formed during the 1980s, coinciding with efforts to define such rights in the United Nations.[20] Another organizing frame that may be displacing the ethnic unity/liberation one is the anti-racism/minority rights frame. Half of the groups listing this as a key goal were formed after 1980, and one quarter was formed during the 1990s. Finally, peace issues continued to be the focus of organizing for a consistent percentage of groups, despite the dramatic changes in the geopolitical situation following the Cold War. And women's issues are also the focus of a consistent percentage of TSMOs.

Beyond influencing the size and structure of the transnational social movement sector, we also must ask whether and how the inequalities in the world system are reflected in transnational activist groups. We would expect organizations based in the rich, core countries to have advantages over those outside the core. For instance, we might expect them to have an easier time gaining recognition from and maintaining ties to other non-governmental organizations and inter-governmental agencies. Greater resources would also allow such groups to incorporate a more geographically diverse membership, thereby enhancing their political voice. Moreover, richer groups should be best able to survive over time. Table 2 compares the extent to which groups in the core and periphery are successful at surviving and cultivating ties to other groups.

The results in Table 2 are mixed. Groups whose members were only from periphery countries were less likely to survive than were groups based in core countries. However, organizations that transcend the North-South divide are the most successful at not only survival but at mobilizing allies. But contrasting our expectations, South-only groups were more likely than their Northern counterparts to maintain formal consultative status with IGOs and to have ties with other NGOs.

Can this be taken to mean that TSMOs have been able to overcome structural inequalities that are entrenched in the global system? Probably not. Ties with international organizations or other external actors are a way for relatively weak groups to increase their access to resources and otherwise enhance their ability to act in the global political arena (Bob 2001). So the data in

---

[20] Brysk (2000); Passy (1999).

Table 2. Recognition and Survival: Comparisons of Core- and Periphery-based TSMOs.

Scope of Member Base	N	Consultative Status w/ IGOs	NGO-links average	IGO-links average	Survival 1993–2000
1993					
South Only	65	40%**	5.4**	2.3**	
North Only	105	19%	3.1	1.0	
Both N. & S.	369	41%***	5.9 e	3.1***	
2000					
South Only	77	49%*	6.3	3.2**	69%
North Only	182	34%	4.8	2.0	82%
Both N. & S.	491	46%	7.7***	3.7***	87%***

   * T-test comparisons of means for North only vs. South only groups significant (p < .05).
  ** T-test comparisons of means for North only vs. South only groups significant (p < .01).
   e T-test comparisons of means for "Both North and South" vs. groups in North or South only significant (p < .05).
*** T-test comparisons of means for "Both North and South" vs. groups in North or South only significant (p < .01).

Table 2 may nevertheless be reflecting weakness as much as strength. First, groups in the North enjoy greater direct access to and influence on the major power (e.g., core) governments, thereby affecting the course of most major policy decisions even without substantial ties to global institutions. Southern activists are doubly disenfranchised, since their home governments are often less open to democratic influences and less able to affect the course of international policy. They are therefore more reliant on transnational alliances in order to redress their grievances.

Ties with external actors can also be interpreted as a weakness because they can undermine the autonomy of an organization. While no effective social movement organization can succeed if it seeks complete autonomy, organizational survival and to some degree effectiveness depends upon an organization's abilities to define and pursue a course of action around which its members are united. If a group has to respond to financial incentives or other pressures from external allies or international agencies, its ability to define and pursue its original goals may be compromised.

Also, while many international agencies share TSMO goals like environmental protection, just economic development, and demilitarization, they are still under the control of collections of states. They often aid groups by providing resources and information and by advising organizers about how best to influence multilateral negotiations. But they also may deliberately seek to co-opt or at least assuage challengers. At the very least they can serve to channel protesters' energies towards institutionalized forms of action (e.g. efforts to monitor and/or shape international treaties), thereby displacing more radical critiques and disruptive forms of protest. The evidence in table 2 shows a need for more detailed case study research to uncover the complex relations between intergovernmental and non-governmental organizations.[21]

Another way to approach questions about how structural power impacts the transnational social movement sector is to ask whether organizations tend to be based in places that favor already privileged, core groups or whether they are accessible to activists in areas outside the core. Looking at the location of TSMO headquarters, we find that the vast majority are in core countries, and that even within those countries, they are concentrated in key cities – such as New York or Geneva – that serve as headquarters for global political institutions and commerce. However, the tendency of TSMOs to locate their headquarters in major global cities appears to be declining somewhat. We also see more TSMO headquarters in the global South. In 1973 just 12% of all groups were based in the South, and by 2000 this figure rose to more than 20%.

An unexpected development we see is that more TSMOs are being organized within regions (see Table 2, column 2). About a third of all groups were organized within either the global North or the South in 2000, whereas this figure was around one-fifth of all groups in 1973. There has been a parallel decline in the percentages of groups that organize across North and South. Seventy-one percent of TSMOs formed before 1990, and just 51% of groups formed after 1990, included participants from both the North and South (t = 4.92). The overall number of trans-regional groups, however, continues to grow, so we cannot say that regional organizations are completely displacing more universal ones. Rather, it suggests a shift in organizing strategy.

Boli and Thomas's analysis of the more general category of international non-governmental organization (INGOs) showed a similar, growing tendency for these groups to organize along regional lines. They argued that regional

---

[21] Cf. Friedman et al. (forthcoming); Cullen (2003).

organizing enjoyed the "practical advantages of shared language, culture, and history as tools for mobilization with respect to the larger world" (1999: 31). In their view, the broader world culture and its institutional artifacts define an overarching framework within which "world culture authorizes and compels organization at diverse levels" (1999: 31–2). Thus, the formation of regional groups has been shaped by the UN global conferences, where negotiating contexts encouraged efforts to build broad consensus among NGO participants. Regional organizing also facilitates consensus-building in global NGO arenas, since activists first work through their differences in more localized contexts where the interests of participants are likely to converge and where power differentials are minimized. In global settings, regional spokespersons can represent the views and interests of their regions as they work with their counterparts to achieve a broader consensus. This interpretation would suggest that regional organizations complement rather than compete with the work of broader TSMOs by helping to bridge local- and regional-level concerns with broader international processes. In other words, such groups may be mobilizing new constituencies into transnational political arenas.

The final question I ask here is how changing technologies that have fueled globalization of economic, political, and social relations have affected the structures of transnational SMOs. The discussion above anticipated that the comparatively greater access to inexpensive travel and communications would produce more decentralized organizational structures. The *Yearbook* data provide support for the expectation that TSMOs would become more decentralized in structure over time. There has been a consistent decline in the percentage of TSMOs organized as centralized federations, that is organizations with national sections that typically share a common organization name and a more formal and centralized decision making structure. Amnesty International is a prominent example of such a group. In the 1970s, about half of all active groups took on the federation form, but by 2000 we find less than 20% adopting this more centralized structure.

The federation form is being replaced by the coalition, probably because the latter structure allows more autonomy for members and facilitates rapid decision making. Making up just one quarter of all groups in the 1970s, coalitions made up more than half the population of TSMOs in 2000. While they vary quite a bit in how they operate, coalitions typically allow affiliates to maintain their own organizational name and affiliation and allow more diversity in goals and strategies of affiliates. Such groups are better suited to rapid decision making at local or national levels, and they encourage innovation by members. The decentralized organizational structure allows affiliates greater flexibility as they seek to address in a local context the organization's collective goals.

This trend towards more decentralized or network-like structures may help to explain the pattern we found in Table 1 of a declining rate of growth in the TSMO sector. The less centralized coalition structure may be able to incorporate a larger number of free-standing national and sub-national groups than is the more hierarchical federation structure. Thus, while the absolute numbers of new TSMOs reveal a slowing growth rate, the level of actual participation in transnational organizations could indeed be on the rise. Additional evidence about membership size is needed to assess this, and such data are not available from the *Yearbook*.

Conclusions

The 1990s witnessed dramatic changes in the global political system as the Cold War bipolar system gave way to greater efforts at multilateral approaches to a wider range of global problems. This study explored whether and how those changes affected the patterns of transnational social movement organizing. We also examined whether structural inequalities in the world system are mirrored in the transnational social movement sector.

While the numbers of TSMOs continued to grow between the early 1990s and 2000, the rate of growth has slowed dramatically from that of recent decades. The size of the sector more than doubled between 1983 and 1993, but its growth rate was considerably lower during the 1990s than in the two previous decades. This finding may be the result of greater competition for members and other resources among this growing population, or it might reflect changes in the broader political system that served to reduce the strategic advantage of transnational organizations. It may also result from a greater ability of transnational coalitions to absorb a larger variety of local and national organizational adherents, thereby streamlining the interest aggregation process at the global level (Murphy 2001). We need more localized data to assess the meaning of this macro-level trend.

A second expectation was that the end of the Cold War would allow for an expanded international issue agenda and would alter the issue focuses of TSMOs. The most dramatic change during the 1990s was that many more groups are organizing around multiple-issues rather than as single-issue groups. This may reflect a greater recognition among activists of global interdependencies and of the relationships between issues such as human rights, environment, development, and peace. Certainly the opportunities for transnational communication and dialogue facilitated by transnational associational structures have helped shape these multi-issue frames. Also, the shift towards greater international trade and towards multilateral trade agreements is paralleled by an expansion in the numbers of TSMOs working on issues relating to economic justice.

Comparisons of core and periphery regions showed some important differences. We expected that periphery regions would be less integrated into TSMO memberships and that they would also have less access to intergovernmental agencies, lower levels of recognition by other NGOs, and lower survival rates. The organizational data we examine bore out some but not all of these expectations. Groups that organized in the global South only were less likely to survive between 1993 and 2000 than were groups in the North. However, groups organized across the North-South divide were most likely to survive, and they were also better able to establish ties with intergovernmental organizations and with other actors in their environments. South-only TSMOs were also more likely than their Northern counterparts to have formal consultative status with an IGO, and they had consistently larger numbers of ties with both IGOs and NGOs. Whether these connections with external actors serve to amplify the influence that Southern activists can have in the global political arena or whether they simply serve to reduce the autonomy of such groups without giving them substantial political benefits is a question that further research should address.

We found some evidence to support the argument that transnational organizations are becoming more widely accessible, and we saw small increases in the percentages of groups based in the global South. One other finding that may have important consequences for the future course of transnational organizing is that a larger percentage of groups are organizing within regions rather than across the North-South divide. A larger percentage of new TSMOs are organized within the global North or South than was true in the past. This may create more opportunities for people to make connections between their local interests and global processes, but it could also complicate efforts to resolve the critical differences between the interests of people in the global North and South that hinder global cooperation on economic, environmental, and security issues. Further research is needed to determine how regional level organizing affects possibilities for broader, trans-regional cooperation.

Finally, we examined the ways that changing technologies have affected the organizational structures of TSMOs. The proliferation of comparatively inexpensive communication and transportation possibilities was expected to enable TSMOs to adopt more decentralized forms. This was indeed the case, and we found a shift from the more centralized federated structure towards more decentralized, coalition structures that allow TSMO affiliates greater autonomy.

In short, we see some important changes in the growth and geographic makeup of the transnational social movement sector. These are likely to affect future possibilities for transnational mobilization, and in particular, the abilities of transnational groups to overcome differences in interests and culture that inhibit transnational organization, particularly across major structural divisions like North and South. This organizational infrastructure has arisen over decades, and its expansion as well as its shifts in issue-focus and geographic makeup suggest that it will continue to provide a basis for nonviolent transnational organizing, despite the setbacks it may have faced in the immediate aftermath of the September 11 attacks.

Appendix. Data Collection Methods

The *Yearbook of International Associations* is edited by the Union of International Associations (UAI) in Brussels, which was charged in an early UN Resolution with helping maintain a census of international associations of all kinds. The UAI identifies organizations that have members in at least three countries through a number of mechanisms, including referrals from other organizations, website searches, and self-identifications. The UAI sends an annual survey to organizations it lists in order to update each entry and to assess whether or not a group remains active (*Yearbook of International Associations*, Annual).

Like any data source, the *Yearbook* has important limitations, especially when one is interested in tracking groups that may be minimally structured and dependent upon volunteer labor. It also under-represents non-state groups that use violence as a political tactic, since these groups are unlikely to seek inclusion in the *Yearbook*, for obvious reasons. The *Yearbook* staff, nevertheless assembles the most complete census of international organizations, and its methods for continuously identifying new groups are rigorous. Moreover,

Yearbook editors update their census annually, and they have incorporated Internet searching into their methods. They indicate both newly formed groups for which they have minimal information as well as indications that a group has ceased activity.

In earlier years, the selection process excluded labor unions as well as "Institutes" and "Foundations" in order to limit the possibilities of including groups that may have government affiliations or whose work involves primarily research or funding activities outside the realm of social movement activity. In the 2000 collection process, we included all of these organizations in order to allow us to examine labor groups and to determine how the prior exclusion of such groups influences our understanding of the sector of organizations advocating social change. Of 1064 organizations identified in the 2000/1 *Yearbook*, 106 or 10% were either labor organizations, foundations or institutes. Most of these (71%) were labor organizations. To maintain comparability with earlier years, however, our analysis here is limited to groups that fall under our selection criteria for the earlier periods, thereby excluding these groups. The groups that are included, then are all nonviolent organizations with members in at least three countries that pursue any kind of social change goal.

Once the population of TSMOs was identified, each listing was coded to record information such as the location of the organizational headquarters, the countries of membership, issue-focus, membership structure, and ties with other nongovernmental organizations (NGOs) as well as with IGOs. Groups were also tracked between the two time periods so that we could identify which groups that were present in the earlier time period disbanded or were otherwise inactive by 2000. This tracking across time-periods also identified some groups that were missed in the 1993 selection process, leading us to update the previously-reported figures for 1993. Additional information about the funding sources of TSMOs was recorded for the 2000 period.

Bruce Podobnik

Resistance to Globalization: Cycles and Trends in the Globalization Protest Movement

Introduction

In the late 1990s, a series of major protests against multi-lateral financial institutions such as the World Trade Organization revealed that broad sectors of world society are opposed to corporate-driven forms of globalization. Analysts of these protest events were impressed by the fact that social groups with histories of tension were increasingly taking part in the same protest actions. Workers and environmentalists, for instance, were observed marching together in the streets of Seattle, Genoa, New Delhi, and Porto Alegre – to name just a few examples. Indeed, this 'blue-green' alliance was taken by many to herald the birth of a new, broad-based social movement of the left intent on resisting elite-driven forms of globalization.

Though generally labeled '*anti*-globalization protesters,' the form of resistance that has emerged to challenge policies promulgated by organizations such as the WTO, the World Bank, and the IMF can more accurately be called the *globalization protest movement*. This is because the vast majority of groups that participate in these protests draw on international networks of support, and they generally call for forms of globalization that enhance democratic representation, human rights, and egalitarianism. Indeed, it is my claim that we have witnessed the consolidation of a new kind of protest movement – one which is incorporating increasingly broad segments of world society into a coherent movement of resistance to the challenges posed by corporate-driven forms of globalization.

The majority of the studies that have traced out the rise of this globalization protest movement have relied on case study analyses of particular protest events. This case-study methodology has produced extremely useful, detailed examinations of the ground-level interactions between, for instance, workers and environmentalists. Thanks to the work of such analysts as Maiba (2001), Panayotakis (2001), and Smith (2001), we now know a great deal about the nature of the alliances that have been forged between different kinds of activists in specific regions of the world.

At the same time, we know less about the broad cyclical and evolutionary trends in the social composition of protest activity over a longer period and at a global level. Though case study analyses demonstrate that workers and environmentalists took part in some of the same protests in the period 1998–2001, for instance, they are not able to show how often this alliance occurred in earlier years. And, indeed, a whole set of related questions cannot be addressed by case study analyses alone. What other combinations of social groups have occurred with regularity in these globalization protests? Which kinds of social combinations are most common? Are global protests more common in certain regions of the world than others? And, finally, are the protests becoming more common on a global level – or has the harsher post 9/11 national security environment succeeded in derailing this protest movement?

This chapter intends to shed light on these questions by carrying out a quantitative analysis of newspaper reports on globalization protests that occurred during the period that stretches from January 1990 through June 2004. By engaging in this analysis, I am able to show that the globalization protest movement has not been fundamentally sidelined by escalating terrorist and military confrontations that have followed the 9/11 attacks. On the contrary, protesters who long mobilized against elite-driven economic policies have been joined by a new contingent of anti-war activists across the world. What had been primarily a confrontation over global economic policies before 9/11, has broadened into a sustained, world-scale contestation over the political and economic projects that should guide the contemporary world.

Data Sources and Methods

The empirical research presented in this chapter is based on a content analysis of newspaper articles drawn from 15 news services over the period January 1, 1990 – June 30, 2004. The articles were downloaded from the Lexis-Nexis news service, an online service that provides comprehensive access to news articles published across the world. The information collected from these articles has been assembled into a regularly-updated database on the globalization protest movement.

As indicated in Table 1, the news services that were searched come from all major regions of the world. Most of these news organizations attempt to achieve multinational coverage, though six specialize in reporting on events in one region only. Taken together, the articles captured from these newspapers provide a uniquely global coverage of the globalization protest movement. Of course, in content analysis research it is never assumed that all relevant events can be captured. Instead, the key objective is to attain a consistent level of coverage over the time period of interest. To the extent that consistency in coverage is achieved, changes in the number or type of events captured can be assumed to reflect changes in the actual phenomenon. By following the procedures outlined below, I am confident that a consistent degree of coverage has been attained in this study.[1]

Table 1. Overview of Globalization Protest Database.

Period of Content Analysis: January 1, 1990 through June 30, 2004.

News Services Searched: Africa News Service, Associated Press, British Broadcasting Corporation, CNN, Daily Yomiuri (Tokyo), Financial Times (London), ITAR/TASS (Russia), Inter Press Service, Japan Economic Newswire, Jerusalem Post, Los Angeles Times, New York Times, Times of London, Washington Post, Xinhua News Service (China).

Search Term Used: (protest! and globali!) or (protest! and (international w/1 monetary w/1 fund)) or (protest! and imf) or (protest! and (world w/1 bank)) or (protest! and gatt) or (protest! and (world w/1 trade w/1 organization)) or (protest! and wto) or (protest! and summit)

Number of Articles Analyzed: 1777

Number of Unique Events Identified: 1178

---

[1] See Gerner, et al. (1994), Silver (1995), Rucht and Neidhardt (1999), and Imig (2001) for demonstrations that systematic analyses of newspaper articles are able to measure patterns in international events.

The initial search called up 1,777 articles from the Lexis-Nexis database. A second selection process was then carried out, in which each of these articles was scanned for reports of protests against the various international institutions that have been targeted by the globalization protest movement.[2] Protests that were exclusively national/local (with no reported international orientation) were excluded. In addition, only protests carried out by civil society groups were included – and so trade disputes between political representatives of governments were excluded from the database. Of the 1777 articles captured in the computerized search, 1556 met the criteria described and were entered into the globalization protest database.

Once the articles had been selected, a content analysis was performed to collect information on each of the unique events reported in the articles. A unique event was defined as an occurrence that took place in the same location over a continuos period of time. If protests were reported to have occurred in separate locations, they were coded as distinct events even if they were carried out in coordination by similar kinds of social groups. If more than a 48 hour interruption was seen to have occurred between actions carried out in the same location by the same group, then a new event was coded as having occurred.

Using these criteria, all events reported in the articles were coded separately. Sorts on location and date were then performed, and all multiple reports of the same events were identified. Final event cases were then compiled that contained the fullest information provided by the multiple articles.[3] Once all available information was consolidated into a single case, the duplicate reports of the event were deleted.

By the end of this process, 1178 unique protest events had been coded into the globalization protest database. These events reflect protest actions car-

---

[2] As indicated by the search phrase, key organizations of interest included the IMF, the World Bank, and the GATT/WTO. A more generic term (summit) also captured protests against a broad range of other organizations, including the Asian Development Bank, the FTAA, the G8, NAFTA, the World Economic Forum, the European Union, and the Summit of the Americas (among many others).

[3] Occasionally, different newspaper articles reported different information on the same event. In cases where discrepant information was provided, two strategies were pursued. If a majority of articles reported a similar piece of information, then that information was coded. Otherwise, the separate pieces of information were coded separately and an average of the estimates was calculated (as with varying estimates of the number of protesters at an event).

ried out in 107 countries, or 329 separate locations, during the period January 1, 1990 – June 30, 2004. Using this empirical data, we can turn to an analysis of the broad trends and transformations in the globalization protest movement – paying particular attention to the shifting global dimensions and social composition of the movement over time.

The Globalization Protest Movement in Broad Perspective

It is sometimes argued that the globalization protest movement took shape in the late 1990s and that it is focused primarily in the advanced industrial world. And there has been a widespread assumption that the new national security context that emerged after the attacks of Sept. 9, 2001, will undermine the movement. An examination of the broad geographic, temporal, and social dimensions of the movement, however, allows for a re-appraisal of these assertions.

The first common assumption about the globalization protest movement is that it is focused primarily in the developed world. As indicated in Table 2, however, events associated with the globalization protest movement are actually concentrated in less-developed countries (LDCs). According to the information captured in the database, for instance, 53% of the 19 million individuals who are recorded as having participated in globalization protests during the period 1990–2004 did so in LDCs. More remarkably, 88% of the reported injuries and 69% of the arrests occurred in LDCs. Finally, of the 901 deaths reported to have occurred during globalization protests over the period, 1 occurred in the developed world (in Genoa) while 900 occurred in LDCs. Clearly, a substantial part of the human drama associated with the globalization protest movement is occurring in the global south.

A closer analysis of the distribution of events by world region[4] reveals other important features of the globalization movement. The most lethal region appears to have been the Middle East, where 405 of the 901 deaths recorded in the database occurred (in Yemen and Morocco, specifically). Latin America follows closely with 366 reported deaths. The region where the largest proportion of protesters were injured was Asia, though Latin America follows closely on this dimension as well. Latin America also registered the highest

---

[4] See Appendix for a description of the world regions used in this analysis.

number of arrests. So far, in other words, LDC regions dominate the picture. Interestingly, however, the region with the largest proportion of protest participants was Western Europe. Meanwhile, a particularly high proportion of arrests were reported in North America (the USA and Canada). In sum, the LDC regions dominate most dimensions of protest activity, though Western Europe exhibits high protest participation levels while North America registered elevated arrest rates.

Table 2. Information on Globalization Protest Events, January 1990 – June 2004.

REGION	# Protesters in Events		# Protesters Injured		# Protesters Arrested		# Protesters Killed	
	Number	% of Total	Number	% of Total	Number	% of Total	Number	% of Total
DCs	9,215,141	47 %	607	12 %	9,312	31 %	1	0.001 %
LDCs	10,213,044	53 %	4,321	88 %	20,341	69 %	900	99.99 %
Total	**19,428,185**	**100 %**	**4,928**	**100 %**	**29,653**	**100 %**	**901**	**100 %**
Africa	1,169,002	6 %	583	12 %	2,177	7 %	100	11 %
Mid East	859,994	4 %	918	19 %	703	2 %	405	45 %
Asia	2,229,844	11 %	1,418	28 %	4,319	15 %	24	3 %
Lat Am	5,079,379	27 %	1307	27 %	11,153	38 %	366	41 %
E Eur	464,194	2 %	81	2 %	667	2 %	1	0.1 %
W Eur	7,751,929	40 %	376	7 %	2,661	9 %	1	0.1 %
Nor Am	956,373	5 %	66	1 %	5,941	20 %	0	0 %
Pacific	917,470	5 %	179	4 %	2,032	7 %	4	0.4 %
Total	**19,428,185**	**100 %**	**4,928**	**100 %**	**29,653**	**100 %**	**901**	**100 %**

Having examined all events combined, let us now turn to an analysis of the temporal patterns of the globalization protest movement for the period from January 1990 to June 2004. When examined at the level of individual countries, it becomes clear that protests against structural adjustment and liberalization policies have occurred with remarkable regularity across the developing world. Throughout this 12-year period, protests have occurred in an average of 20 developing countries each year (ranging from a low of 13 in 1991 to a high of 30 in 2001). In addition to this relatively constant level of turmoil in individual nations, however, two truly global patterns can be discerned. The first reflects a constellation of protests surrounding periodic GATT/WTO negotiations, and the second reflects a sustained upsurge in unrest since mid 1999 that appears to mark the onset of a new era in globalization protest activities.

Figure 1 allows for an investigation of these global patterns of unrest. As demonstrated in the figure, citizens in the less-developed world have been mobilizing with remarkable consistency against neoliberal policies throughout the 1990s.[5] By far the largest number of protest events, and the largest mobilizations of people, have taken place in the global south. Meanwhile, citizens in the global north contributed on occasion to protests in the first half of the decade.

Figure 1. Globalization Protest Dynamics, January 1990 – June 2004.

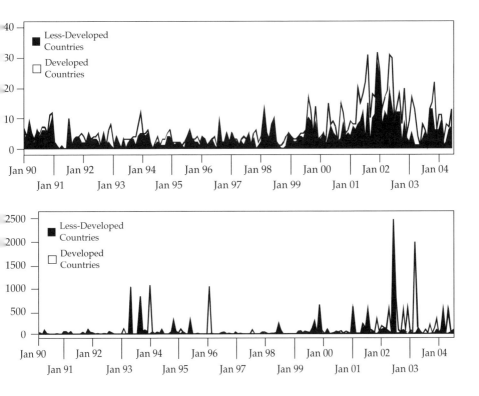

---

[5] As Walton and Seddon (1994) have demonstrated, protests against the IMF and World Bank emerged as an important international phenomenon in the 1980s. My database does not currently cover this earlier period.

One of the most intriguing aspects of figure 1, though, is that it reveals a sustained upsurge in protest activity after January 1999 in both the global south and north. This wave of globalization protest activities appears to reflect a distinctly new social dynamic. To begin with, the kinds of people engaging in these protests broadened significantly in both the developed and developing regions of the world. Whereas workers and farmers formed the backbone of protests throughout most of the 1990s, more recent events have seen growing participation by students, environmentalists, human rights advocates, and indigenous groups (see below for a closer analysis of these social transformations). Moreover, the geographic scope of the protests grew, until it seemed that no sizeable summit could be held in any region of the world without attracting serious unrest.

During the period between mid 1999 and Sept. 11, 2001, the globalization protest movement was entering a new phase in which mobilizations were occurring with increasing frequency and the events themselves were resulting in higher-impact outcomes (both in physical and media terms). And then came the events of Sept. 11, 2001, and an escalation in national security and military crises across the world. To many it seemed as if one modest challenge to world-systemic stability, the globalization protest movement, was suddenly displaced by another, far more menacing threat. But has that been the case?

As shown in figure 2, there was a brief pause in protest activity in both developed and less-developed regions of the world right at the time of the attack. Immediately after the attacks, protest organizers in the global north called off a number of planned actions or else re-cast them as anti-war demonstrations. A particular concern of US organizers was that, in a new era of perceived vulnerability, the violence which sometimes accompanies globalization protests would turn public opinion against the movement (Wayne 2001).

Peaceful protest actions, with significant participation by self-proclaimed globalization activists, did re-emerge quite rapidly in Western Europe though. In early October 2001, for instance, a march of approximately 300,000 people was held in Perugia, Italy, while another anti-war/globalization protest demonstration involving almost 100,000 people took place in Brussels in December. By the early months of 2002 similar anti-war/globalization protests involving hundreds of thousands of citizens had taken place in Barcelona, Madrid, and Seville. This anti-war/globalization wave continued to grow as the Bush Administration prepared to invade Iraq, so that in the first months of 2003

Figure 2. Globalization Protest Dynamics, January 1999 – June 2004.

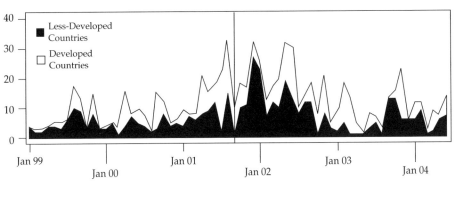

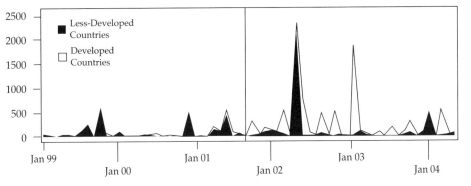

an estimated 15 million citizens across the global north marched in the name of peace.

The pause in globalization protests in the global south was also quite brief. In early November 2001 over 10,000 citizens in Ankara, Turkey, demonstrated against IMF-imposed austerity measures. At the same time, more than 30,000 farmers marched in the streets of New Delhi to protest threatened reductions in agricultural protections. Then, during November 2001, large protests against the WTO meeting in Qatar were undertaken in Tanzania, South Africa, Hong Kong, and Qatar (with smaller protests against the WTO meeting also taking place in Berlin, Paris, London, and Washington DC). Through the first half of 2002, meanwhile, globalization protests involving tens of thousands of people were mounted in Brazil, Honduras, India, Nigeria, Turkey, and Venezuela. And, the turmoil engulfing Argentina makes it stand out dramatically in the database. Indeed, according to the events coded into the database, from August 2001 through June 2002 over 2 million people took part in austerity protests in Argentina. The resignation of numerous heads of state and financial leaders demonstrated in stark terms the capacity that protests have to generate significant political change at the national level.

It is also possible to measure the post-9/11 endurance of the globalization protest movement by examining the size of protests at the annual summits that have become targets of activists. As shown in Table 3, there has been no appreciable decline in the number of people amassing at the barricades surrounding meetings held by the WTO, the IMF/World Bank, the G8, or the World Economic Forum. Indeed, the fact that somewhere between 40 and 50 thousand people took to the streets in Washington DC in 2002 to criticize the IMF, the World Bank, and the US government provides additional evidence that the globalization protest movement remains vibrant even in the United States.

Table 3. Number of Protesters at Summit Events.

	World Trade Organization Ministerials	
1998	Geneva, Switzerland	2,000–3,000
1999	Seattle, USA	50,000–70,000
2001	Doha, Qatar	1,000–1,000
2003	Cancun, Mexico	2,000–3,000
	IMF/World Bank Annual Meetings	
1998	Washington, USA	2,000–3,000
1999	Washington, USA	1,000
2000	Washington, USA	7,000–10,000
2001	Washington, USA	Cancelled
2002	Washington, USA	40,000–50,000
2003	Washington, USA	1,000
2004	Washington, USA	2,000–3,000
	G8 Summits	
1999	Berlin, Germany	8,00–1,000
2000	Okinawa, Japan	25,000–30,000
2001	Genoa, Italy	50,000–60,000
2002	Calgary, Canada	2,000–3,000
2003	Evian, France	25,000–27,000
2004	Savannah, USA	1,000–2,000

Table 3 (*cont.*)

	World Economic Forums	
2000	Davos, Switzerland	1,000
2001	Davos, Switzerland	2,000
2002	New York, USA	3,000
2003	Davos, Switzerland	1,000
	World Social Forum	
2001	Porto Alegre, Brazil	20,000–30,000
2002	Porto Alegre, Brazil	40,000–60,000
2003	Porto Alegre, Brazil	70,000–75,000
2004	Bombay, India	80,000–90,000

From the vantage point of almost three years after the 9/11 attacks, it therefore appears that the globalization protest movement has sustained its momentum. While partly reflecting a few uniquely large mobilizations against austerity programs in countries like Argentina and Zambia, this upsurge also reflects the massive anti-war/globalization protests that have swept around the world in 2003 and 2004 (see figure 3). Moreover, this multi-faceted movement has also generated a crucial space within which alliance-building and strategizing activities can be undertaken. Growth in attendance at the World Social Forum meetings suggests that the movement is developing an organizational structure that can help it negotiate the challenges of integrating very disparate social groups into a common struggle against the neoliberal and national security projects of the world's elite.

Figure 3. Major Protest Events, Jan 1999 – June 2004.

NUMBER OF PROTESTERS

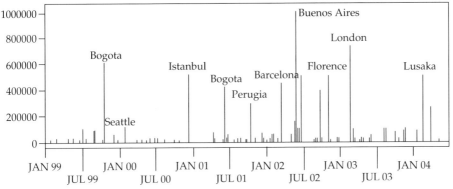

Social Transformations in the Globalization Protest Movement

As stated earlier, there is evidence that the kinds of people engaging in globalization protests broadened significantly after January 1999. Whereas workers and farmers formed the backbone of protests in the earlier part of the 1990s, more recent events have seen a significant increase in activism by environmentalists, students, youth, members of non-governmental organizations, human rights advocates, peace activists, and other social groups. Indeed, figure 4 demonstrates the increased frequency in which more that one distinct social group has participated in a specific event after January 1999.

Figure 4. Numbers of Distinct Social Groups Reported at Event.

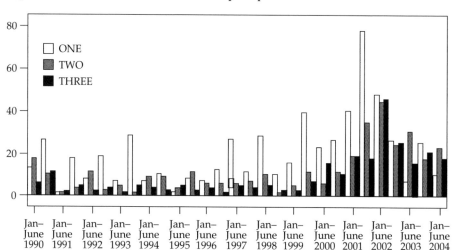

To examine changes in the social composition of globalization protests, I have utilized a specific procedure to merge the many different kinds of protesters described in newspaper articles into a manageable number of groups that can be subjected to analysis. The first section of Table 4 shows the nine categories that all protesters have been sorted into. It is important to note that many news reports do not fully document the different kinds of people participating in events, and so an analysis of protester types can only be suggestive. However, I do believe it is possible to discern broad transformations in the social composition of protest event by examining the terms used by reporters and activists.

Table 4. Frequency of Protester Types in Events.
January 1990 – June 2004

EXAMPLE TERMS FROM NEWS ARTICLES	ANALYTIC CATEGORIES USED
ANTI-GLOB/IMF/WB/WTO ANTI-G8/EU/APEC/WEC & OTH SUMMITS ANTI-CORPORATIONS/CAPITALISM	**ANTI-GLOB**
ENVIRONMENTALISTS	**ENVIRON**
NGOS HUMAN RIGHTS CHURCH	**NGO**
STUDENTS YOUTH	**STUDENT**
FARMERS PEASANTS/INDIGENOUS	**FARMER**
PUBLIC SECTOR WORKERS (ALL KINDS) PRIVATE SECTOR WORKERS (ALL KINDS)	**WORKER**
ANTI-WAR ANTI-USA	**PEACE**
DEMONSTRATORS (NOT OTHERWISE SPECIFIED) CITIZENS (NOT OTHERWISE SPECIFIED)	**UNSPECIFIED**
UNEMPLOYED/RETIREES BUSINESS SECTOR POLITICIANS/POLICE/MILITARY GUERRILLAS	**OTHER**

PERCENTAGE OF EVENTS IN WHICH PROTESTER CATEGORY INVOLVEMENT WAS REPORTED

Workers (all types)	39%
Demonstrators/Citizens (unspec)	32%
Anti-Globalization, etc.	23%
Farmers/Peasants/Indigenous	16%
Environmentalists	15%
NGOs/Human Rights/Church	11%
Students/Youth	10%
Peace	9%
Other	8%

Table 4 (*cont.*)

FREQUENCY OF PROTESTER TYPE COMBINATIONS IN DATABASE*

Combination	Number of Events in Which Combination was Reported
Environ & NGOs	60
Students & Workers	44
Anti-Glob & Workers	38
Environ & Workers	38
Farmers & Workers	37
Anti-Glob & Environ	35
NGOs & Workers	33
Peace & Workers	31
Environ & Farmers	28
Anti-Glob & Anti-War	26
Anti-Glob & NGOs	24

All other possible combinations reported in less than 20 events each.

---

* Data should be treated with caution, as there are likely to be many un-identified categories of protesters in news reports of events.

Table 4 then maps out the number of times each major type of social group was reported to have participated in globalization protest events. As revealed in the second part of the table, workers from the private or public sector are by far the most commonly-identified actors in globalization protests during the period January 1990 – June 2004. Protesters against multi-lateral organizations such as the IMF, the World Bank, or the WTO, are the second most commonly reported category, followed then by while farmers, environmentalists, NGOs, students, and peace activists. Meanwhile, figure 5 shows that workers and farmers are mentioned as participants in events throughout the 1990s – while all the other categories begin appearing in news reports primarily from the late 1990s on.

Clearly, there are two broadly different social dynamics in operation in these globalization protests in both the north and south. On the one hand, worker and farmer organizations have consistently engaged in defensive actions against trade liberalization throughout the period of analysis. And on the other hand, a more diverse group of new social groups from the political left began to mobilize against corporate-driven forms of globalization after January 1998. These newer participants in globalization protests have gained a great deal of analytic attention in recent years, but it should be noted that they are joining an already well-established tradition of globally-oriented activism forged by workers and farmers from across the world.

Figure 5. Types of Protesters Identified in Events, January 1990 – June 2004.

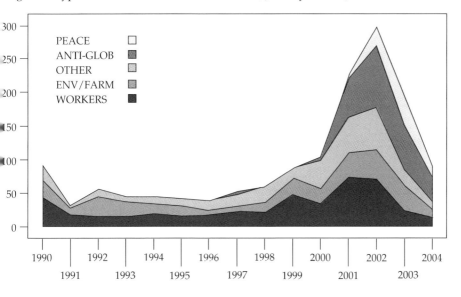

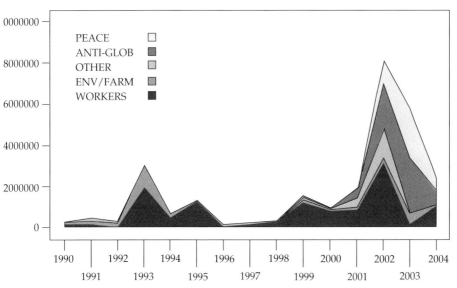

In addition to examining the distinct kinds of social groups that have participated in globalization protest events, it is also intriguing to analyze whether these groups participate in separate or joint mobilizations. The final section of Table 4 lists the number of times in which specific actor combinations were reported to be present in protest events. What is particularly interesting here is the fact that the much-discussed worker/environmentalist combination emerges as being one common – but not the most common – grouping. Instead, joint participation by environmentalists and NGOs/human rights/church groups in protest events is by far the most frequent grouping. Surprisingly, the combination of students and workers is also quite common, as is the combination of so-called anti-globalization protesters and workers. Note the frequency with which workers appear in conjunction with another social group. It would appear that workers across the world are participating alongside many other kinds of social actors in globalization protests.

Of course, it is an open question as to whether or not different kinds of activists coordinated their efforts in any particular protest – even if they did end up marching side by side. In some cases mobilizations were quite spontaneous, and little cross-group communication occurred. In other cases, distinct kinds of activists worked together extensively to create large-scale, high-impact protests. The creation of alternative summits – such as those held in Porto Alegre – has facilitated this process of cross-communication and cooperation between different groups (Amin 2002). It may be that, in the context of these kinds of inclusive events, truly enduring linkages can be forged between various social groups that have traditionally engaged in their own distinct protests against corporate-driven forms of globalization.

It is important to highlight that mass mobilizations carried out by specific kinds of activists, or by coalitions of protesters, have already generated important results at regional and global levels. As documented in Table 5, at least eight governments have been overthrown due entirely or in part to pressures exerted by grassroots campaigns. In 70 other instances, moderate to severe political crisis have been created by these protests – and many government officials have been forced to resign their office. Meanwhile, in over 50 cases IMF austerity programs and World Bank projects have been cancelled, delayed, or revised because of mobilizations. And at least 24 global summits/trade meetings have been significantly disrupted. The fact that many of these high-impact events have occurred since the 9/11 attacks underscores the reality that the globalization protest movement continues to exert a significant effect on the contemporary world-system.

Table 5. Results of Protests (When Reported).
January 1999 – June 2004

Result	Number of Events
Government Overthrown in Part b/c of Protests	8
Difficulties/Crisis Created for Leaders	70
Talks Held between Protesters and Leaders	19
Leaders Acknowledge Protester Concerns	14
Austerity/Liberalization Program Eased	30
IMF/World Bank Project Delayed/Cancelled/Revised	24
Meetings Disrupted	24
Meetings Held in Remote Location	6
Total Number of Events with Discernible Result	198
Total Number of Events	1178

Countries/Years in which Government was Replaced due in Part to Protests:

Lebanon (1992), Sao Tome (1992), Thailand (1997), Ecuador (1997), Indonesia (1998), Ecuador (2000), Argentina (2001), Bolivia (2003).

Countries/Years in which Serious Political Difficulties were Created by Protests:

Romania (1990), Ivory Coast (1990), Trinidad (1990), France (1990), South Korea (1990), Thailand (1990), Philippines (1990), Guyana (1991), Barbados (1991), Romania (1991), Costa Rica (1991), Panama (1991), Venezuela (1992), Guatemala (1993), Nigeria (1993), South Korea (1993), India (1994), Bangladesh (1994), Sudan (1995), Haiti (1996), Argentina (1996), Bulgaria (1997), Argentina (1997), Zimbabwe (1998), Yemen (1998), Romania (1999), South Korea (1999), Thailand (1999), Ecuador (1999), India (1999), USA (1999), Argentina (2000), Turkey (2000), Argentina (2001), Italy (2001), Indonesia (2001), Bolivia (2001), Argentina (2002), Italy (2002), Peru (2002), Ecuador (2002), Dominica (2002), Zambia (2002), Dominican Republic (2003), Ecuador (2004), Zambia (2004).

Conclusion

This analysis provides a quantitative overview of the broadest features of the globalization protest movement. By examining newspaper reports from across the world, I have shown that the protests mounted against elite-driven processes of globalization have been a consistent feature of the world-system throughout the 1990s. In both the global north and south, an increasingly broad set of groups have mobilized themselves to challenge what are perceived to be unfair or anti-democratic forms of economic liberalization and restructuring. Indeed, this study demonstrates that important transformations have occurred in the social components that make up the globalization protest movement. The dominance of workers and farmers of the early 1990s gave way to a much more diverse set of activists after about 1998. Since then, groups with long histories of rather acrimonious interactions have increasingly taken to the streets together in both the developed and developing worlds. In addition to the rise in worker/environmentalist combinations, my analysis highlights the rise in combinations such as students/workers and NGOs/workers. This suggests at least the possibility that different components of the political left are forging new linkages that can allow for more effective, globally-oriented forms of activism over the medium to long term.

Appendix. Countries in Regional Categories

The 8 regional categories used in the globalization database are defined as follows: *North America* includes Canada and the USA; *Latin America* includes Mexico, the Caribbean, Central America, and South America; *Africa* includes sub-Saharan Africa; the *Middle East* includes Northern Africa, as well as the Persian Gulf area; *Western Europe* includes the wealthier nations of Central Europe which have become affiliated with NATO and the OECD; *Eastern Europe and Central Asia* include all of the area that was formerly part of the Soviet Union; *Asia* includes South Asia; and the *Pacific* region includes Australia, New Zealand, Japan, and the other wealthy East Asian nations. The 2 global categories used are defined as follows: *Developed Countries* includes 24 countries from North America, Western Europe, and parts of the Pacific region; *Less-Developed Countries* includes 81 countries from Latin America, Africa, and Asia. For more information on these categories, or on any aspect of the research presented, please contact the author.

Lesley J. Wood

Taking to the Streets Against Neoliberalism: Global Days of Action and Other Strategies

Introduction

We live in an era when international financial institutions like the World Trade Organization, the International Monetary Fund, and the World Bank continue to promote a neoliberal form of globalization. In response, a broad coalition of protest organizations has formed to challenge this agenda on a global scale. But, it is not yet clear what kinds of tactics work best against international institutions. When the target is the global neoliberal project, to whom do activists direct their anger and their claims? And how have their tactics changed since September 11, 2001?

This chapter aims to shed light on these questions by examining characteristics of protest against neoliberal institutions that were carried out during the period 1998–2002. The analysis suggests that we must investigate pre-existing protest traditions, social movement networks, and diffusion processes if we are to arrive at an understanding of the dynamics of contemporary anti-globalization protests.

My research shows that, while the most visible targets of anti-globalization protests have been the World Trade Organization, the International Monetary Fund and similar institutions, these events are only the tip of the iceberg.[1] On 'global days of action,' for instance, local events have been organized in over 100 cities. These protests targeted a wide range of institutions – including banks, stock exchanges, local and national governments, McDonalds restaurants, and Nike stores. And though they were spread across wide areas of the world, these coordinated protests share important characteristics. Indeed, if we examine these targets of protest using a broad frame of analysis, we can see important underlying patterns in operation.

The Emergence of Transnational Protest Strategies

Historical research has demonstrated that protest techniques spread across the world as changes in political conditions evolve. The consolidation of nation states in nineteenth century Western Europe, for instance, created new challenges and opportunities for those who were striving to carry out social change. At that time, protesters shifted their focus away from local authorities, and toward national leaders who were amassing political influence. This shift in targets was also accompanied by a change in tactics – away from somewhat spontaneous and often violent actions, and toward more organized, non-violent "repertoires of contention." Increasingly, the timing of protest came to be tied to the rhythms of parliamentary discussion and governmental action.[2]

Despite occasional changes in dynamics of mobilization, the repertoires of protesters have remained surprisingly stable over the past century. Indeed, protesters who mounted challenges to national governments in the 1960s were drawing on many of the same tactical strategies that were developed in the nineteenth century. However, there is evidence to suggest that the more recent shift in power toward transnational institutions requires the development of new strategies of protest. Protest techniques that were useful against specific nation-states are possibly not as effective in our increasingly globalized world. Many analysts argue that this shift in political realities is prompting a corresponding shift in repertoires of protest, away from isolated, domestic protests and toward internationally-coordinated actions that target emerging centers of power at the transnational level.[3] We are therefore witnessing a

---

[1] See Smith and Podobnik, this volume, for similar conclusions.
[2] Tilly (1995, 1997) introduced the concept of the repertoire of contention, and has examined the diffusion of protest strategies over space and time.
[3] Smith (2001); Tarrow and McAdam (2003); Tarrow & Imig (2001).

shift of historic proportions, as social movements try to move beyond influencing policies at the nation-state level to target transnational centers of power.

The first strategy used in this effort to intervene at the transnational level relied on lobbying activities. Beginning in the 1970s, a class of experts emerged that specialized in gaining influence within institutions such as the United Nations, the World Bank, and the International Monetary Fund. Many studies of global resistance focus on the lobbying, conferencing, and networking efforts that have taken place within transnational institutions.[4]

Although certainly important, this lobbying strategy has significant limitations. Groups that have limited access to professional and financial resources are generally excluded from this type of mobilization. Instead, resource-poor groups derive much of their effectiveness from their ability to disrupt business as usual from the outside.[5] For this reason, a new strategy that relied on street-level demonstrations was developed which permitted a wider array of social groups to express their opposition to neoliberal policies. And not only did these demonstrations begin to attract larger numbers of participants; they were coordinated so that protests were carried out at the same time in many different locations.

The international coordination of protest activity began to occur as early as 1998, when the first 'global day of action' was carried out. From then until September 11, 2001, these kinds of demonstrations steadily increased in number and size. But after the attacks on the World Trade Center, there were a number of shifts. Summit protests became less visible, and global days of action became less common. Many North American and European activists distanced themselves from anything associated with violence and intensified policing strategies also dampened protests.

While protests against neoliberalism have at least temporarily declined in the north, it is important to note that unrest is still on the rise across the rest of the world. In fact, the movement against neoliberalism has segued into an even larger set of protests against the war in Iraq. On February 15th, March 15th, and March 22nd 2003, for instance, global days of action were called in which people in over 700 cities took part. Although the driving issues may have shifted, it is still clear that globalization protests continue to be undertaken in the post 9/11 period.

---

[4] Rucht (2001); Tarrow (2002).
[5] McAdam (1982); Piven & Cloward (1979); Tarrow (1998).

My chapter focuses on these more contentious types of transnational protest. I have compiled information on 467 protest events, which took place in 69 countries on five global days of action between 1998 and the end of 2001.[6] My analysis will mostly emphasize the protest patterns in the pre-9/11 period. But, I will also survey events that have been undertaken since 9/11, and will describe continuities and divergences in recent patterns of contention.

Factors Underlying the Rise of Global Days of Action

Global days of action are not new. In 1889, the Socialist International declared May 1st to be a day of workers' demonstrations. Labor Day is an important time of worker mobilizations across most of the world to this day. In 1910, a similar process led to the establishment of International Women's Day. The next year, more than one million women and men attended simultaneous rallies in Austria, Denmark, Germany and Switzerland in the name of improved women's rights.

Though it has deep historical roots, the strategy of 'global days of action' has become increasingly utilized in the past five years. This strategy encourages local activists to protest on a specific day in their own communities, but against a commonly-defined opponent. The dates I am examining generally correspond with summits of transnational institutions such as the IMF, the World Bank, or the World Trade Organization. Targets have also included international financial institutions, McDonalds, Nike, genetic engineering and, most recently, the war against Iraq. While my analysis focuses primarily on the global days of action organized against the summits of international financial institutions, wider dimensions of the phenomenon will also be discussed where appropriate.

Let me begin by reviewing key conceptual tools that are useful in shedding light on the rise of global days of action. Previous research has demonstrated that organizations generally choose tactics that conform to existing traditions of activism in a particular region and on a specific issue. Tactics

---

[6] Events were included in the dataset if they affiliated themselves with the global day of action through speeches or signs, or if they submitted a report to compilers of protest activities against transnational institutions. Repeated 'google' searches from 1998–2004 for 'protest,' 'action,' 'demonstration,' WTO, IMF, World Bank, G8 and the abbreviations for the dates, "M16, J18, N30, S26 and N9" built this collection, with the goal of a complete set of events. Fortunately, activists had already compiled lists of many of these events. Sites were viewed during August 2004.

and targets are also selected in response to changes in the structure of political power.[7] Just as the rise of the nation-state prompted a shift in activist tactics, there is now evidence to suggest that the shift of power to the transnational arena demands the development of new mobilization strategies.

Social movements have long engaged in independent struggles against certain aspects of the neoliberal agenda. Advocates of sustainable development have targeted the World Bank, while anti-debt activists have focused on the IMF, and so on. These kinds of campaigns have tended to be carried out as separate organizational efforts. Recently, however, activists have begun to see how their interests are connected, and that joint mobilizations are required in the current era. A recent trend has therefore emerged in which a great variety of groups are linking their struggles together, into a common front against neoliberal forms of globalization. By uniting together in networked ways, anarchists from Europe can broadcast stories about their successful "street party" protests, while they in turn hear tales of the Zapatista resistance. At the same time, unionists and environmentalists can learn from each other's strategies, while the struggles undertaken in communities across the global north and south can be linked in new ways.[8]

This process has been described as *scale shift* – meaning a change in the number and level of coordinated actions.[9] Tarrow (2002) has noted that scale shifts result from at least two related processes. First, new protest strategies tend to diffuse to new sites along pre-existing network connections. And second, groups that are already linked in some broad coalition tend to adopt similar approaches and protest strategies. These related processes not only facilitate the building of new coalitions, but they also spread new conceptual definitions of allies, opponents, and tactics. While a lot more research needs to be done on each of these dynamics, my own analysis in this chapter focuses specifically on how new protest strategies against neoliberalism diffused through pre-existing networks.

The spread of social movement strategies depends on activists being able to creatively adapt new tactics, messages, and targets. This innovative capacity itself depends in part on the existence of networks that link movement organizations (Chabot et al., 2003). For instance, the organization ATTAC has

---

[7] Tarrow (1998); Steinberg (1999); Mische (2003).
[8] The "north" here is defined in terms of economic influence and includes the southern hemisphere countries of Australia and New Zealand.
[9] McAdam et al. (2001); Tarrow & McAdam (2003).

activist centers in France and Germany, and strong links between these centers. This helps explain why ATTAC activists in each country tend to employ similar tactics in their marches and protests.

In addition to examining network connections between protesters, we must also look at relationships that exist between civil society and political institutions. Protest practices tend to spread at comparable rates through regions of the world that are structurally equivalent.[10] Research has shown that similar types of protest move through countries of the global north, where citizens have a certain degree of access to organizations like the IMF or the World Bank. Other kinds of protest flow through countries of the global south, where the distance between citizens and international institutions of power is much greater (Walton & Seddon 1994). So, to understand the variation in protest tactics and targets we also need to consider the relationships between sites of protest and the structure of global political power.

In summary, there are a number of key factors that influence the ways protesters in different regions of the world carry out actions against neoliberal institutions. We must consider pre-existing repertoires of contention, the nature of social networks, and the structures of power that exist in different regions of the world. As I turn now to an empirical analysis of a particular kind of neoliberal protest, we will see how these factors interact to generate patterns and variations in protest activity.

An Empirical Analysis of Global Days of Action

My analysis is focused on a new style of protests that have been mounted against neoliberalism. These protests were held on or around five days designated as "global days of action," which took place between 1998 and the end of 2001. The first was called by the People's Global Action Network for May 16–18, 1998, to coincide with the meeting of the G8 in Birmingham and the meetings of the WTO in Geneva. The Jubilee 2000 network also participated in these mobilizations. During this global day of action, 43 protest events were held in 41 cities across the world.

The following year, on June 18, 1999, a second global day of action was called against the G8 meeting in Koln, Germany. Similar organizations were

---

[10] Soule (1997); Tilly (1997).

involved in planning and coordinating the protests. In the end, 58 mobilizations took place in 54 cities against the G8 meetings.

The third global day of action was called for November 30, 1999, against the WTO meetings in Seattle. This is, of course, the most well known of all global days of action. A large number of organizations participated in the action, and as a result the mobilizations were unprecedented in their size and scope. In fact, 111 distinct protest events, in 97 cities around the world, are recorded as having been undertaken against the WTO during this global day of action.

The fourth global day of action was called against the meetings of the IMF and World Bank in Prague, and grew to involve 98 protests in 88 cities. The last day in my dataset was conducted against the meetings of the WTO in Doha, Qatar, and included 157 events in 152 cities – which makes it the most geographically diverse day of action to that date.

Unlike many studies of contentious events, I make use of activist reports of protest events that are gathered from the Internet. This approach improves upon standard strategies of using news media as a source. I identified 467 events that took place over the 5 days of action, while a Lexis-Nexis search of all news media identified only 127 events and a Reuters search only captured 40 events.[11] The activist reports provided more details on tactics and events than traditional media reports. The media accounts also tend to over-report violent events. And, finally, different pictures of event size tend to emerge depending on sources. Activists appear to emphasize larger numbers when they report on their events, while news media are more likely to accept lower police estimates.

Events are included in my analysis if they involve more than 10 people, and are explicitly identified with a global day of action. Organizational meetings or conferences are excluded. Events that have been included include rallies, leafleting, marches, street parties, property destruction, street theater, civil disobedience, riots, occupations, banner hangs, a guerilla attack on a police station, and the disruption of offices, businesses, and streets. Interestingly, 27 of the events identified by the traditional news media were not included

---

[11] Coverage for the November 9, 2001 event includes one reference to "30 events in Germany", and a list of 19 cities where events were planned by the Canadian Labour Congress. Evidence suggests that some of the Canadian events were primarily educational, and would not have been considered contentious events in our data. They were excluded unless other reports gave more details.

in activist reports. This suggests that some events were carried out by isolated activist groups, and were missed by the larger networks. But, they were monitored by the media and authorities. These 'missing' events were equally spread across time and continents.

These global days of action were called by various activist networks, such as Jubilee 2000, the International Confederation of Federated Trade Unions, and the People's Global Action network. Meanwhile, the largest mobilizations in these actions were those that targeted the WTO. And while the majority of demonstration events occurred in Europe and North America, it is important to note that Asia and South America witnessed the largest events in terms of people involved.

While the majority of protests symbolically target the relevant global institutions on the given day, most protesters actually direct their ire at local institutions. The most popular local target is the multinational corporation, while national governments, banks and stock exchanges also attract significant amounts of opposition.

It is also important to note that, while these protests are being coordinated by many different organizations, there may be little cross-organization agreement on ultimate goals. For instance, there is disagreement about whether the WTO and organizations like it should be reformed or abolished (Smith 2001). Networks aiming for WTO reform include the International Congress on Federated Trade Unions, the Jubilee 2000 network, and the ATTAC organization. Each one demands improved consideration of labor, debt relief, and financial equality issues in WTO negotiations.

Meanwhile, a host of more radical organizations call for the abolition of the WTO. The People's Global Action network, for instance, calls for a ". . . rejection of capitalism, imperialism and feudalism – and all trade agreements, institutions and governments that promote destructive globalisation."[12] Similarly, "reclaim the streets" protests in Europe, North America, Australia,

---

[12] Launched in 1998 in Geneva, the PGA is a decentralized collaboration with no formal membership, linking existing organizations that have endorsed the hallmarks. The network is active in approximately 40 countries, particularly in Latin America, Asia and Europe. Participants include the Sandinistas, Zapatisas, Phillipine, Brazilian and Indian Peasant Movements and the European direct action movement including Britain's Reclaim the Streets and Italy's Ya Basta. The demonstrations organized by groups identified as part of the PGA (through inclusion on the PGA webpage) make up 53% of our dataset. http://www.nadir.org/nadir/initiativ/agp/en/index.html. Sites were viewed during the summer of 2002.

and New Zealand tend to involve those who are openly hostile to international financial institutions and global capitalism.[13]

The changed political climate after 9/11 led to an increase in the proportion of protest events affiliated with networks interested in reform, while anti-capitalist protests appear to decline in number. In the case of ICFTU and Jubilee networks, this reflects a shift back to nationally oriented protests and the lobbying of transnational institutions. ATTAC has shifted some of their energy into anti-war demonstrations, and the PGA has decentralized in its decision-making to the regional level. Some PGA affiliates have continued to promote more radical tactics.[14]

In addition to having distinct goals, different networks focus on specific targets. A slight majority of protests (52%) were directed against international financial institutions like the WTO, the IMF and the World Bank. Labor federations, ATTAC and Jubilee 2000 tend to focus on these specific targets. In contrast, demonstrations affiliated with the PGA network, or related networks like Reclaim the Streets, were more likely to select a local corporate or political target. Indeed, 226 of the 467 demonstrations made claims against a concrete target other than the transnational institutions explicitly under protest.

The most popular local targets were the branches and headquarters of multinational corporations. McDonalds, Nike, Monsanto, the Gap, Shell and others were focuses of protest in twenty-seven percent of the events in my sample. In Canada, the US, Europe, Australia and New Zealand, activists are more likely to target a corporation than any other local target. Interestingly, these are the countries most central to the neoliberal institutions. These are also the countries that are most likely to lack established repertoires for fighting against neoliberalism. After the 1999 protests of Seattle, this targeting strategy diffused quickly to new sites of protest on these continents.

Although stores were targeted in the US during the civil rights movement, these more recent anti-corporate protest tactics appear to have emerged from

---

[13] As McCarthy has pointed out, a primary goal of many transnational social movement organizations may be to build transnational solidarity beyond state boundaries (McCarthy 1997, 72).

[14] The global conference of the PGA took place as scheduled from September 19–22nd, 2001 in Bolivia. However, the post 9/11 political climate made travel for the delegates difficult for a number of reasons. Delegates were refused visas and permission to travel. The Bolivian government denounced the PGA as a 'terrorist summit'. The Executive Intelligence Review published the article 'Terrorism Central: People's Global Action.' During a press conference held by the PGA, journalists questioned the relationship between the PGA and the terrorist attacks (Sophie 2001).

recent environmental and anti-sweatshop activism traditions. But what is the logic behind targeting a corporation that is not accountable in any directly democratic manner to the public? Writer Naomi Klein offers one explanation. She argues that these targets are not the real goal. "For years, we in this movement have fed off our opponents' symbols – their brands, their office towers, their photo-opportunity summits. We have used them as rallying cries, as focal points, as popular education tools. But these symbols were never the real targets; they were the levers, the handles. They were what allowed us . . . 'to open a crack in history'" (Klein 2001).

Protesters often argue that, when they target a specific McDonalds, they are also targeting globalization, corporate control, the WTO, capitalism, and the USA. They also often explain that they are fighting for animal rights and labor rights, as well as against rainforest destruction. Or they argue that McDonalds itself is the problem. Indeed, McDonalds appears to have become a universal but multi-dimensional symbol for globalization.[15]

Although corporations were a common target before 9/11, there is some evidence to suggest that they may be less frequently a focus of protest after that key event – at least in the US and Canada. Before 9/11, up to forty-nine percent of protests on a particular day of action targeted corporations. On November 9th 2001, the figure was only 10%. Since that time, actions called against corporations like Procter and Gamble, British Petroleum and McDonalds have attracted fewer numbers of protesters.

Meanwhile, nineteen percent of protest events in the sample targeted national governments. In Africa and Asia, protests were more likely to target national governments than any other target. Interestingly, none of the countries that had high levels of targeting national governments were in the G8. Counter-intuitively, this suggests that the most powerful governments in the world are less likely to be targeted by their populations – while peripheral governments are more likely to be the focus of protests.

Although the recent linking of anti-globalization and anti-war mobilizations has again focused protester attention on governments, my dataset cannot reveal whether a sustained shift toward a focus on governments has occurred. Still, it does appear that European protesters, at least, continue to target their domestic political authorities (Tarrow 2001). And if we look glob-

---

[15] McDonalds was a target at 25 protests in my dataset.

ally it is possible to state that national governments continue to be targets of protest in Latin America, Asia and Africa.

Interestingly, fifteen percent of the protests in the sample targeted banks and/or stock exchanges. There was an increase in the proportion of protests that targeted banks on the second day of action, June 18th, 1999, due to the 'Global Carnival Against Capitalism's' call to action by the PGA network, which explicitly identified financial centers as targets. In Latin America, banks and/or stock exchanges are the most frequent local targets.

This pattern is related to pre-existing repertoires. Latin American social movements have been fighting against the structural adjustment policies of the IMF and World Bank for over twenty-five years. Massive riots in the 1970s and 1980s built a history of protest against privatization and neoliberal reforms. Governments and opposition groups routinely blame the IMF for all manner of problems, and direct the attention of the public to appropriate targets (Walton and Seddon 1994, 133).

It appears that when choosing local targets, protests tend to target the historically resonant and accessible symbols of transnational power. The influence of new forms of protest is tied to these pre-existing repertoires. The targets of protest shifted dramatically in the US and Canada after 9/11 away from corporations, and toward the transnational institutions themselves. In most of Latin America, though, protest routines continued as before. I should add that in Argentina there was a sharp increase in protests against banks in the 2002–2003 period.

Overall, it is clear that pre-existing domestic groups transpose contention to the international level without entirely ending local or national types of protesting (Tarrow and McAdam 2003). This is one reason why there are distinct patterns in protests and targets from one region to another. In order to understand why the targets of anti-globalization protests differ on each continent, we need to look at pre-existing repertoires, diffusion dynamics, and the political structures of power in specific regions.

The first stream of resistance to the IMF and World Bank began in developing countries, where resistance to IMF-imposed structural adjustment policies became particularly common.[16] Many of the countries that were most active in these protests in the 1970s and 1980s did not participate in more recent global days of action (Robbins 2004). However, those that did participate

---

[16] Walton and Seddon (1994); Smith (2001).

had pre-existing repertoires from earlier austerity protests. In Latin America, the protests targeted the IMF and World Bank, which had long been the primary agents of austerity policies (Walton & Seddon 1994). These institutions continue to be key targets in global days of action throughout the global south.

In contrast, the IMF and World Bank have had little direct impact on populations in the global north. Instead, the WTO and multinational corporations have attracted more attention from activists. So, when northern activists began to engage in global days of action, the WTO and corporations continued to be targeted in North America, Western Europe, Australia, and New Zealand. Overall, it is clear that peoples in different regions of the world continue to draw on their own protest traditions even as they join in new coalitions.

We can also see some regional differences emerge in the post 9/11 period. The changed political climate prompted many activists and groups in the global north to distance themselves from more radical and confrontational forms of protest. For instance, a Jubilee USA network press release from April 2004 explained that crowds at the annual protests against the IMF and World Bank were likely to be less disruptive than they have been in the past. "We're planning a more festive kind of event, with speakers and music and various games with a political point- in the spirit of what is called the festival of resistance," said David Levy, a spokesman for Mobilization for Global Justice (Holly 2004). On the other hand, protests in the global south continue to focus on institutions such as the IMF and the World Bank, and often utilize the same kinds of radical tactics as have been employed in the past.

Concluding Thoughts on the Impact of 9/11

The attacks that were launched against the United States on September 11, 2001, were destined to have some kind of impact on globalization protests. Indeed, some analysts predicted that all contention would dissipate in the new political climate that emerged after the attacks.

Still, only two months later, on November 9, a massive global mobilization took place against the Qatar meetings of the WTO. In fact, the rallies and marches that took place in at least 152 cities worldwide represent what appears to be the largest globally coordinated protest ever held to date. At those demonstrations, crowds chanted against the WTO and railed against their own governments, while others occupied the headquarters of banks and corporations and disrupted commercial outlets. So, it is clear that, on a global level at least, protesting against neoliberal forms of globalization continued after 9/11.

However, there are apparent regional differences in protest dynamics. Specifically, fewer protesters in the United States have targeted corporations. And while anti-war protests have grown in this country, anti-globalization protesting has become less overtly contentious in the US. On the other hand, anti-corporate and anti-capitalist actions continue to be undertaken in Europe and elsewhere. Meanwhile, protests in the global south against privatization and neoliberal reforms have become increasingly intense since 9/11 (Ellis-Jones 2003).

From Brazil to Boston, protesters against neoliberalism continue to reflect their different locations, affiliations and political histories. It is clear that there is no single way to target neoliberalism, and that tactics are continually in flux. As protests against neoliberal forms of globalization continue, we can be sure that new oppositional strategies will continue diffuse across the world. It is also likely that global days of action will continue to be used as a key tactic in the years to come.

Gianpaolo Baiocchi[1]

The Workers' Party and the World Social Forum: Challenges of Building a Just Social Order

Introduction

On the evening of January 24th, 2003, Luis 'Lula' Ignacio da Silva, the former metalworker and founder of the Workers' Party (PT), walked on to the stage at the World Social Forum's largest event as Brazil's President. He told the audience of tens of thousands that he had wondered whether it was appropriate for him to attend the Forum at all. As one of the Forum's early advocates, Lula had himself defended the idea that the World Social Forum ought to be a space for people from civil society – and not invaded government or political party officials.

Now, as Brazil's President, he felt that it was inappropriate to attend as a full-fledged participant. Instead, he emphasized that he was simply playing host to the tens of thousands of people who had come from across the world. Flanked by well-known PT leaders, Lula gave an impassioned speech that called for international solidarity for his efforts to set Brazil on a new developmental trajectory. He closed by promising he would not deviate "one comma" from his socialist ideals. The crowd went wild and started to chant their support.

Lula's attendance at the Forum raised a number of complex issues. The World Social Forum has been

---

[1] I wish to acknowledge the assistance of Gopa Chakravartty, Mark Brenner, and the anonymous reviewers of drafts of this chapter.

hailed by many as one of the most important innovations in global social justice activism. The annual meeting has created a space in which popular alternatives to neoliberal forms of globalization can be created.[2] Activists and scholars have argued that the World Social Forum is a novel "movement of movements" that transcends traditional features of social movements. Indeed, it has been argued that the Forum represents a novel political experiment that is capable of challenging dominant forms of globalization and resisting an emergent form of empire.[3]

Lula's electoral victory in 2002 also represents something quite novel. In addition to the rupture it represents with traditional Brazilian politics, it also reflects the beginning of a new era for the left in Latin America and elsewhere. Lula's tenure as president holds the potential to become a wide-ranging experiment in deepening Brazil's democracy, while expanding the "boundaries of the possible." This includes the possibility that the power of this important nation-state can be used to challenge many of the negative characteristics of neoliberal forms of globalization.

In a sense, Lula and the Workers' Party officials who shared the podium at the World Social Forum were looking out on their mirror image in the multitude of global justice activists. Lula was a social movement activist turned president. And while the gulf separating the PT from civil society groups is indeed real, Lula's new position of power holds out the possibility that new relations can be forged between government and civil society reformers.

Analysts have long created a rigid distinction between the "multitude" and the "party." These kinds of distinctions are particularly evident when the World Social Forum is discussed. The role of the PT in helping forge the Forum is often either downplayed, or the presence of the PT is taken as evidence that social movement spaces are being colonized by hierarchical political parties.

For example, Hardt expresses misgivings about the PT presence in Porto Alegre. He describes a divide between the "parties vs. networks" forms of organization that he believes are present at the WSF. For Hardt this dichotomy represents the gulf between hierarchical parties and non-hierarchical movements. Klein (2003) similarly claims that the large attendance at Lula's speech is evidence of the "hijacking" of the WSF, and that the Forum is therefore

---

[2] Cf. Cattani (2001); Fisher and Ponniah (2003). See also the site of the World Social Forum: http:Forumsocialmundial.org.br.

[3] Hardt and Negri (2000); Wallerstein (2002).

destined for the failure. Others complain that the presence of the PT representatives on the organizing committee of the WSF threatens the autonomy of the Forum, since they believe that "the politics of the traditional left-wing has been to dominate and co-opt the movement of movements" (Adamovsky 2003).

In contrast, I maintain that these kinds of analyses reflect a misunderstanding of the nature of the PT and its relationship to social movements in Brazil. This chapter offers a corrective to these perceptions, by providing an analysis of the history of the PT and its connections to social movements. The objective is to shed light on the PT's potential for crossing the "movement-party divide."

The World Social Forum is far from being a failed experiment. And the Workers' Party is still attempting to widen the scope of civic participation in Brazilian politics. As the party embarks on its first experiment with national power, its deep social movement connections offers an opportunity to bring new imagination to domestic and international policies. Of course, the exigencies of national governance are certain to produce tensions within the PT-social movement alliance. However, there is at least a possibility that both the PT and the World Social Forum can cooperate in their efforts to create a socially-just alternative to dominant forms of globalization.

The History of the Workers' Party[4]

There is a long tradition in the academic literature of arguing that political parties are inherently hierarchical in nature, and prone to co-opt grassroots organizations.[5] Of course, there have been many instances in which political parties have come to dominate and distort civil society campaigns. However, it is at least conceivable that the relationship between a political party and civil society can be more than instrumental. In fact, I would argue that, with the Brazilian Workers' Party, we find a very different kind of party/civil society relationship. This unique relationship has arisen out of a long history of grassroots mobilizations that first created the PT, and then brought it to increasing prominence.

The Workers' Party has evolved from a pro-democracy movement of opposition, into a more traditional party which has amassed a great deal experience

---

[4] See Baiocchi (2002) for a more detailed analysis.
[5] Lipset (1997); Piven and Cloward (1979).

in government. Over this history, the party's key successes can be attributed to the strong, supportive relationships it has forged with civil society groups. The PT therefore breaks from the model of traditional Brazilian politics, which is characterized by hierarchical forms of patronage and personalism.[6]

While formally founded in 1980, the idea of the PT emerged in 1978–79 as strikes were being carried out in Sao Paulo's industrial region. Strike leaders, including Lula da Silva, began discussing the possibility of creating a new "party of and for workers." The idea resonated with trade union activists, and with dissident intellectuals (Singer 2001).

At the time, independent trade unions did not exist and autonomous political parties were largely illegal. Widespread dissatisfaction with the populist Brazilian Labor Party, as well as with the country's old left, fueled this search for a new political space. Meanwhile, increasingly vibrant new social movements, such as those linked to the progressive wing of the Catholic Church, demanded a new arena within which activists could coordinate their efforts. What was needed was an organization that rejected bureaucratic norms, and instead provided a space where "social movements can speak" (Oliveira 1986: 16). After a long period of discussion, a party based on principles of grassroots democracy, mass participation, and socialism was created. It came to be called the Workers' Party (PT).[7]

The founding members of the PT included industrial workers, Christian activists, leftist intellectuals, and pro-democracy activists from a variety of social movements. These original members envisioned the party as a "reflex" of social movements (Ozai 1996). As a result, the PT made use of novel forms of organization and decision-making processes. An open representational structure was created, and distinct groups were encouraged to develop consensus positions regarding party positions and programs. Although internal disagreements were actually encouraged, the coalition was usually able to unite around basic, common positions at times of electoral contests.[8]

The party played a central role in the successful union struggles of the late 1970s. It then further enhanced its status in the following decade by playing a key part in the pro-democracy movement. According to Meneguello (1989), it was during this time that the PT started to broaden its focus beyond working

---

[6] Keck (1992b); Meneguello (1989).
[7] Garcia (1991); Singer (2001).
[8] Cf. Meneguello (1989), Keck (1992a; 1992b) , Harnecker (1994) , Sader (1986) , and Singer (2001).

class issues. Earlier slogans such as "work, land, and liberty" began to be seen as too restrictive. The party instead developed new platforms dealing with social issues, civil liberties, and broader economic justice.[9] By the mid 1980s the PT had come to represent a wide spectrum of social movement interests. This broad alliance then supported PT candidates as they attempted to win municipal and national offices across Brazil.

The Party in Power

Throughout the late 1980s, the Workers' Party steadily gained a foothold in Brazil's political system. By the early 1990s, citizens in 36 cities had elected PT leaders as their mayor. Importantly, Porto Alegre and São Paulo were included in this number, which brought about 10 percent of Brazil's population under municipal PT administrations.

The experience of running mayor's offices and other local administrations forced the PT to confront the challenges of forging new relationships between the party and civil society. Once in power, PT leaders faced a number of difficult choices in their quest to carry out progressive changes. Administrators were constrained by fiscal crises, antagonism from higher levels of government, pressures from local elites, and demands from the party's own constituencies. Also, radical factions of the party tended clash with PT administrators who were perceived to be too moderate. According to Utzig (1996), newly elected administrators faced the difficult task of moderating their own base supporters, as they tried to represent the interests of broader groups in their cities. It was particularly difficult for PT leaders to insulate themselves from wage demands being articulated by their union supporters, even though severe financial difficulties were occurring in most Brazilian cities (Couto 1994).

Many of these early PT administrations collapsed under the weight of these contradictory demands. In fact, a full third of the first generation of PT mayors abandoned their positions before the end of their term, and another third failed to win re-election. But, by the mid 1990s, the PT had become more adept at negotiating the difficult challenges posed at the municipal level. Most importantly, the PT leadership learned that it had to seek out broader bases of support among the underprivileged, rather than relying on

---

[9] Beozzo and Lisboa (1983); Lowy (1987).

its traditional sources of support in the labor community.[10] The learning experiences provided by the early failures of PT administrations therefore set the party on an important new trajectory of evolution.

The second generation of PT administrators increasingly began organizing public forums, to which members of local communities were invited to articulate their desires and negotiate with other interest groups. This forced civil society groups to strive to reach compromises, which diminished the anger directed at the PT administrations. By bringing conflicts into participatory settings, administrators found ways to generate consensus around a new platforms. In the end, the programs that emerged from this process responded to concerns of many groups, rather than just to the agendas of the core bases of PT support. One thing that became clear was that, when city administrators solicited broad grassroots input on what kinds of projects should be undertaken, the resulting policies were likely to thrive.

The best example of this participatory approach to governing comes from the city of Porto Alegre. The PT administration in Porto Alegre succeeded in bringing several thousand people into a number of public conferences regarding the city budget. In the Participatory Budget citizens were able to articulate their ideas about budget priorities – and they were forced to confront trade-offs that had to be made in difficult financial circumstances. This public input proved to be invaluable. In its first four years, the PT Porto Alegre administration succeeded in balancing municipal finances without provoking a political crisis. In subsequent years, the PT administration used its legitimacy with grassroots groups to embark on more ambitious reforms, such as introducing tax schemes that were targeted at wealthier citizens.

Since its first round of meetings in 1989, this approach of convening citizen forums has expanded into new arenas. Throughout Porto Alegre, delegates from civic groups such as neighborhood associations meet to discuss, prioritize, and monitor financial allocations in each city district. The fora have authorized funding for infrastructure projects, new social services, housing, and primary and adult education. In addition, the conference approach has been used to bring citizens into conversations about local cultural projects and broader economic development campaigns. Once projects are initiated, citizens are then also able to participate in commissions that monitor the projects.[11]

---

[10] Jacobi (1995); Pontual and Silva (1999).
[11] Abers (2000); Baiocchi (2002).

At the same time, many PT administrators have become wary of letting participatory programs turn into simple public works programs. Instead, administrations in Belém, São Paulo, Belo Horizonte, and Porto Alegre have fostered participatory programs that are tied not to the provision of services, but instead address broader social and political issues. For instance, municipal conferences have been convened on topics such as AIDS, human rights, women's equality, and racial discrimination. As a result, the PT has shown itself willing to delve into a variety of new issues, rather than remaining focused on the bread-and-butter issues that are traditionally associated with workers' parties.

This participatory experiment has been so successful in Porto Alegre that PT administrations in many other cities have adopted similar programs. The overarching conclusion drawn by the PT is that broad-based participation has the potential to generate support for governmental projects. Indeed, the success of these kinds of participatory projects have contributed to the steadily increasing numbers of PT administrations. These projects have also transformed the party's relationship with civil society.

In the course of its twenty years of experience in government, the PT has shifted its ideological emphasis toward this approach to participatory democracy. The party has utilized these strategies to incorporate and validate the demands of social movements and citizens, without co-opting them. As a result, the base of support for the PT has broadened over time (Trevas 1999). The PT has also experienced a significant renewal in its leadership, as many new activists have risen through the ranks to become party leaders.

The history of the PT in power shows that the party can carry out government reforms in a participatory manner. Initial attempts to rely on the party's core bases of support, such as unions, proved disastrous. But the participatory programs that were developed later proved to be much more successful. This broad-based approach has not only transformed the PT's relationships with civil society, but it has changed the nature of the party itself. The PT has developed a new, cooperative attitude toward Brazilian social movements. And, as we will now see, this new relationship between the party and the multitude has deeply influenced the characteristics of the World Social Forum.

The World Social Forum

According to Bernard Cassen, a leader of ATTAC, the idea of the World Social Forum was developed by European anti-globalization activists. These activists then approached the Porto Alegre administration, and asked whether the event could be held in that city (Cassen 2002). Once approval was granted, activists from Europe and Brazil worked together to create a set of events in which civil society organizations could gather and begin articulating alternative visions of a globalized world, to help replace the neoliberal agenda that was being pushed by international centers of power.

The first World Social Forum, held in January 2001, proved to be a remarkable success. From rather humble beginnings, it grew to include over 100,000 attendees. These participants took part in countless workshops, lectures, testimonials, and networking events. This first World Social Forum is credited with having helped build enduring links between grassroots organizations from many different regions of the world.

After the first Forum, a charter was written to describe the aims of the WSF. The charter states that the WSF is "an open meeting place for reflective thinking, democratic debate of ideas, formulation of proposals, free exchange of experiences and linking up for effective action . . . by groups and movements in civil society that are opposed to neoliberalism and domination of the world by capital" (quoted in Fisher and Ponniah 2003). To protect this space for civil society groups, the charter also explicitly restricted participation by members of official government representatives and political parties.

In subsequent years, the WSF steadily expanded in size, and in the kinds of workshops that were organized. The 2002 and 2003 WSF events were also held in Porto Alegre, and by 2003 similar fora were also being held in Europe, Asia, and Africa. Also, a number of allied events now took place along side the WSF, including the World Education Forum, the Forum of Local Authorities Against Social Exclusion, and the World Judicial Forum.

The city of Porto Alegre was chosen as the location of the WSF three years in a row partly for practical reasons. The municipal government was very supportive of the event, and the city's familiarity with participatory meetings created a helpful context. The city and state government, under encouragement of PT officials, also contributed significant resources to the WSF.

The choice of Porto Alegre also had symbolic meaning. The city had become celebrated as a model of participatory governance, and its approach provided an important model for activists who were trying to identify alternative forms of governing. It was also a city in which a redistributive project had been guided and transformed by a style of radical democracy and discussion from below.

While there were clear reasons for anti-globalization activists to choose Porto Alegre, it is less clear why the local government has agreed to host repeated WSF meetings – especially since this implies costs to a financially-strapped city government. One motivating factor is that such a gathering brings the local PT administration international publicity and solidarity. But another reason why the Porto Alegre PT administration agreed to consecutive WSF meetings is that the party had come to value open-ended discussion and participation by broad sectors of civil society. The WSF is run on the same kinds of inclusive, self-regulating, and non-partisan norms that underlie the city's own budgetary and governing practices, so there is a natural affinity to the event in Porto Alegre.

The sponsorship of the WSF is also related to a broader support of these kinds of fora within the Workers' Party. For instance, in July 1990 the PT administration of Sao Paulo sponsored an international meeting of leftist organizations which became known as the *Foro de Sao Paulo*.[12] This event grew to include over 48 communist and socialist parties, as well as unions and social movement organizations from all across Latin America. While the *Foro de Sao Paulo* has not achieved the size or scope of the World Social Forum, its organization and goals share some affinity with its larger counterpart. Specifically, the *Foro* affirms the value of democracy, social justice, and the need to resist neoliberal forms of globalization. The principal difference is that the *Foro de Sao Paulo* allows formal political parties and government officials to participate, while the WSF restricts participation to civil society representatives.

Overall, the World Social Forum grew to maturity in a supportive context provided by Porto Alegre and the Workers' Party. The successful development of a participatory form of government, and the radically democratic relations that existed between administrators and civil society in the city, offered a hopeful model to activists from around the world. Clearly, the PT and the WSF have each benefitted from hosting a growing effort to create an alternative form of social organization on a global level.

---

[12] This forum was originally known as the meeting of Parties and Organizations of the Left in Latin America and the Caribbean. See the site http://forodesaopaulo.org.

Future Prospects for the PT and the World Social Forum

Although many analysts draw a clear distinction between formal political parties and grassroots organizations, the experience of the Workers' Party in Brazil suggests something different. In this case at least, the distance between the party and the multitude is a lot smaller than appears at first sight. In fact, the experience of the Workers' Party in Porto Alegre has come to represent a hopeful alternative – one in which parties and grassroots groups from civil society collaborate to fashion egalitarian economic and social programs. This model has also significantly influenced the organization of the World Social Forum, and has thereby echoed across the world.

The radical participatory project of the PT, honed through its turns in government, is one that does not seek to bring social movements under the tutelage of the party. Rather, this participatory engagement facilitates discussion among local civil society groups, and thereby allows compromises to be developed.

This form of radical democracy depends crucially on protecting the autonomy of grassroots groups. PT administrators have recognized this challenge, and have instituted policies that are meant to ensure the independence of civil society groups. At participatory budget meetings, for instance, PT members are not allowed to participate as official members of the party. If they do engage in discussions, they do so as independent citizens or as members of civil society organizations. Rules prohibit the meetings from being turned into partisan spaces.

A similar dynamic occurs at the World Social Forum. Once again, PT members are allowed to take part in the event, and they are centrally involved in the organizing work for the WSF (Cassen 2002). However, efforts are undertaken to prevent members of the PT from dominating the events. To date, there is little evidence that PT members have excluded civil society groups or dominated discussions held at the WSF.

It is important to keep in mind that members of the Workers' Party generally began their activist and political careers by engaging in work with independent social movements. Once in the PT, most members retain their affiliations with these grassroots groups. So, they can legitimately wear two hats: that of a member of social organization, and that of an official member of the PT. This partly explains why PT members are frequently in the majority at participatory meetings at the municipal level, and even at the WSF. But this does not mean that the PT controls or dominates these events. It simply reflects the high degree of civic engagement of the individuals themselves. With specific safeguards in place, it appears that the PT is succeeding in developing a participatory model that protects the autonomy of civil society and the sources of innovation it may bring.

On the other hand, a host of new challenges are emerging as the Workers' Party continues to occupy the Presidency of Brazil. For instance, Lula da Silva's economic agenda is turning out to be less radical than many sectors of society want. Rather than overturning trade agreements, or ending relations with international financial organizations, Lula is instead attempting to negotiate for better terms. The Lula administration has also decided to comply with certain IMF conditionalities, and it has raised interest rates in an effort to help domestic capital accumulation. The pragmatism of the administration has already angered leaders of many social organizations, especially since these policies are raising the cost of living for many sectors of Brazilian society.

Indeed, during the 2005 meeting of the World Social Forum, many participants took Lula's administration to task for its perceived capitulation to the neoliberal agenda. The position of the Workers' Party is particularly vulnerable at this stage, and its long-term prospects are somewhat uncertain.

It is useful to remember in this context, though, that the PT stumbled when it first assumed power at the municipal level. Chastened by its initial failures, the party was then driven to create a new model of governance at the mayoral level that proved to be quite successful. There is evidence to suggest that the PT will try to replicate this transformation at the national level, by creating new spaces in which competing social groups can provide unmediated input on things like national budgetary priorities. Whatever the outcome of such an effort, it is immensely important that the PT be able to learn about the challenges involved in progressive national governance. This PT experiment is not only relevant to citizens in Brazil, but it can also provide insights for all those who oppose neoliberal forms of governance – and are looking for alternative responses to globalization.

Whatever the fate of Lula's administration, it is undeniable that the World Social Forum continues to provide an invaluable space in which progressive movements can forge new connections and visions of the future. The WSF is certainly not dominated by the PT at this point in time. In fact, its independence from the party has grown as Lula's administration has generated grassroots antagonism. Currently, then, it appears that the PT's long-term goal has been achieved. The party invested resources and energy in fostering autonomous spaces for discussion and negotiation, and now its role in these spaces has been circumscribed. Social movements would not have a space in the WSF to appropriate were it not for the early institutional support and vision of the party.

Many activists realize that, until a very different framework for globalization emerges, grassroots struggles will have to be carried out in a world that is dominated by national governments and traditional forms of politics. In the case of the Brazilian PT, we find an example of how new, interactive relationships can be forged between political parties and social movements. Those who are involved in the quest for social justice must continue to re-imagine the possibilities that exist in this contradictory space between formal politics and grassroots mobilizations.

The history of the PT, and the recent experiences of the World Social Forum, demonstrate that it is not necessary to create a sharp distinction between "the party and the multitude." Instead, new efforts must be undertaken to develop participatory models of governance that work at the municipal, national, and even international levels. Only by engaging in this work can we hope to avoid a future in which political parties and social movements alike are swept away by much less democratic forces.

Thomas Hall and James Fenelon[1]

Trajectories of Indigenous Resistance Before and After 9/11

Introduction

In the late nineteenth century, Thomas Jefferson Morgan, Commissioner of Indian Affairs in the United States, predicted that "the great body of Indians will become merged in the indistinguishable mass of our population."[2] This was expected to occur as a result of national policies that were meant to destroy, displace, or absorb indigenous peoples into the dominant US society. These policies were not only undertaken in the US in the nineteenth century. They instead reflect a global process of forced incorporation that has been underway for many centuries. Indeed, nation-states across the world have been attempting to eradicate or assimilate native peoples for at least five thousand years (Chase-Dunn and Hall 1997).

Interestingly, more than a century after Morgan's prediction it is clear that indigenous peoples are not only "still here," but they are one of the fastest growing segments of the population of the United States.[3] At

---

[1] This chapter is considerably revised from an original version, which appeared in the Journal of World-Systems Research (volume 10, issue 1). For more details, we suggest readers see this earlier version or our forthcoming book, Hall and Fenelon (in press a). We have developed parts of this argument in various papers given since 1998. As is typical, we owe a great deal to the many scholars who have commented on these efforts, especially the editors of this volume. Remaining problems and errors are our responsibility.

[2] Iverson (1999); Cadwalader and Deloria (1984).

[3] Snipp (1992); Nagel (1996).

the global level, indigenous peoples continue to exist in sizeable numbers.[4] The fact that indigenous peoples have not yet been obliterated raises an important set of questions. How have indigenous peoples survived the pressures of global capitalism on a broad level, and the efforts by national and regional authorities to forcibly incorporate them in particular countries? And, what are the prospects for continued survival in the new global security environment that followed the Sept. 11, 2001, attacks?

Indigenous survival may appear to have little relation to 9/11 and the "war on terrorism." However, we argue there are important ways in which the two connect. First, it is clear that many indigenous movements have become participants in the broad-based "anti-globalization movement" that has arisen to challenge the expanding global capitalist system. To the extent that more intense security reactions are undertaken by states against this anti-globalization movement, indigenous groups may be subjected to more severe forms of coercion and repression. Second, indigenous movements have also been drawn into a variety of ethnic conflicts across the world. As national and global elites increase their efforts to contain ethnic conflict, attacks on indigenous groups may increase. And, finally, the "war on terrorism" could transmute into a new, virulent form of Manifest Destiny in which the United States seeks to export its form of democracy, neoliberalism, and consumer culture to the entire planet. Once again, the unique heritages and autonomy of indigenous communities across the world may be in ever-greater danger in the contemporary period.[5]

In order to examine the prospects for protecting the survival and resilience of native peoples, it is important to place recent threats in a broader historical context. Our chapter is intended to carry out this kind of world-historical analysis. We begin our investigation with a comparative analysis of some of the ways indigenous peoples have survived long-term threats to their existence. We then review the challenges indigenous groups pose to an expanding capitalist system, and to conceptions of sovereignty embedded in the modern inter-state system. And, finally, we examine the impact of the 9/11 attacks and the new national security environment on indigenous groups across the world. It is our conviction that, by arriving at a better understanding of successful instances of indigenous resistance, we can learn important lessons

---

[4] Wilmer (1993); Smith and Ward (2000); Bodley 2003.
[5] Wickham (2002); Dunaway (2003b).

about how the contemporary capitalist world-system can be transformed into a more diverse and humane global system.

Examples of Indigenous Resistance to Global Capitalism

Indigenous resistance to the expansion of empires and states has taken place throughout human history.[6] But the creation of the capitalist world-system in sixteenth-century Europe, and its subsequent expansion to ever-wider reaches of the world, subjected indigenous communities to new challenges. What seems to be unique about the capitalist world-system is the ever-growing demand for new resources, labor, and new markets that lies at its core. Moreover, the need to strengthen national governments that are located in a competitive inter-state system has led to much stronger attempts to assimilate groups than was common in the pre-capitalist era.

The creation and then steady expansion of the global capitalist system has exposed indigenous peoples to intense threats. Within this long historical process, many distinct strategies of destroying or assimilating indigenous groups have been employed. Genocide – the outright murder of members of an identifiable group – has been used extensively. At the same time, more subtle efforts to destroy a group's ethnic identity (ethnocide), and culture (culturicide) have also been employed in efforts to wipe out arenas of resistance and autonomy.[7]

So how is it that indigenous peoples have resisted processes of genocide, ethnocide and culturicide? Indigenous resistance to global capitalism is a world wide and very diverse phenomena.[8] As Scott's (1985) analysis of the 'weapons of the weak' has demonstrated, many forms of indigenous resistance are covert and secretive. Accidents of history, like relatively small populations and/or relative geographic isolation, have often aided survival. Controlling resources that are thought to have no or little value to the larger system has also helped at times. Some indigenous communities, in other words, have managed to persist on the margins of the capitalist world. In other

---

[6] Chase-Dunn and Hall (1997); Hall (2002).

[7] This discussion draws heavily on the work of Fenelon (1997, 1998) who developed the concept of culturicide. Clastres (1980) makes the earliest use of the term ethnocide, albeit not with this precise meaning.

[8] The category, "indigenous peoples," itself is a gross simplification of an immense variety of types of social organizations. See Hall and Nagel (2000).

circumstances, though, native resistance has been quite overt and dramatic – and has been mounted within the heart of the system.

For instance, the rebellions that have taken place in Chiapas, Mexico, have often been cast as a revolt by peasants against new economic threats unleashed with the 1994 adoption of NAFTA. But the rebellion is also part of a much longer-lasting movement of indigenous Mayan resistance against national and global processes of incorporation.[9] Indeed, once we know to look for it, it becomes clear that indigenous groups are undertaking defensive struggles in all regions of the world. In the United States, the American Indian Movement can be seen partly as an indigenous movement of resistance. Meanwhile, the Saami are mounting similar challenges in Europe. And, across Asia, Africa, and Latin America, indigenous peoples have continued to mount quite significant challenges to dominant national and global elites.[10]

These movements are so diverse, and so fluid in their modes of organization and goals, that they all but defy summary. But we can say that one thing that distinguishes indigenous movements is their emphasis on local community ties, land claims, and rights to carry out a variety of "traditional practices." These traditional practices may include maintaining the communal ownership of resources, forming unique kinds of families, reserving specific pieces of land for sacred ceremonies, and other activities. Many of these practices contradict, challenge, or even threaten the values embedded in capitalist and state-based systems.

For instance, the communal ownership of resources has often come into direct conflict with the concepts of private property that are at the core of the capitalist world-economy. Contrary to what many colonizers, missionaries, and development experts have assumed, it is not that indigenous people do not understand the concept of individual ownership. Rather, they have long recognized that resources are always partially, if not wholly, "public goods," and thus many people rightly have claims over those resources. The ability of indigenous peoples to forge linkages with environmentalists derives in large part from a deep agreement on this alternative concept of ownership (Gedicks 1993, 2001).

Another form of resistance has involved efforts to maintain "traditional culture." Here, we see traditional culture not as a static and unchanging

---

[9] Instances where Chiapas is seen as an indigenous movement may be found in McMichael (2003); Boswell and Chase-Dunn (2000); Collier (1999), among other sources
[10] The literature on indigenous forms of resistance is quite large. See: Perry (1996), Smith and Ward (2000), Gedicks (2001) for examples.

phenomenon, but rather as evolving according to the desires of group members.[11] Again, once we know to look for it, we can see cultural forms of resistance being carried out in all parts of the world. For instance, tribal colleges in the United States provide a space in which indigenous languages, histories, and identities are being revived and reinvigorated (Boyer 1997). Similar, alternative education systems, are flourishing in many other regions of the world as well.

Religious traditions provide another important space of opposition. The revival of traditional practices like the Sun Dance and the Longhouse religion, along with revitalization movements such as the Ghost Dance and the Native American Church, have helped indigenous communities in the United States resist assimilation.[12] Their survival and growth, near the very heart of the system, is an important testament to the power of indigenous groups to sustain unique identities and cultures in the contemporary period.

Religion generates lines of contestation in another important way as well. Many indigenous peoples attach deep spiritual significance to specific lands. This often leads to conflicts between those who prioritize the extractive utilization of eco-systems, and those who want to protect its natural integrity. Fights also emerge over the ownership of such resources. Whereas capitalist, state-based systems define ownership in terms of private property, many indigenous communities emphasize communal access to resources (Champagne 2003, 2005; McLeod 2001). One of the more dramatic examples of this kind of conflict is the effort of Lakota peoples to regain control of the Black Hills in the United States. Multiple courts have determined that the territory of the Black Hills was illegally taken from the Lakota peoples (Churchill 1996; Lazarus 1991). In accord with U.S. law, the settlement of this property conflict was to have been achieved through monetary payment to the affected parties. The Lakota peoples, however, have refused monetary settlements and have instead insisted on the return of sacred land to the entire community. The fact that the Lakotas involved in the dispute live in the poorest county in the United States underscores the intensity of commitment to protecting communal and sacred spaces.[13]

---

[11] Fenelon (1998); Smith and Ward (2000).

[12] Wallace (1969); Jorgensen (1972); Brown (1976); Thornton (1986); Stewart (1987); Fenelon (1998); Iverson (1999).

[13] The county in question is Shannon county, South Dakota, where the Lakota Pine Ridge reservation is located.

Running through many of these conflicts is the issue of sovereignty. Indeed, claims of indigenous sovereignty are the basis of challenges to the power of states around the world. In fact indigenous movements regularly call into question the structure and legitimacy of the modern interstate system (Wilmer 1993).

Although native peoples have often met with some success in maintaining sovereignty, they have had to fight on European grounds – using European law. Recently, one of the more outstanding successes has been to use the doctrine of sovereignty to build gaming operations that have, at least in some locations in North America, generated considerable profits.[14] It is unclear, however, how much indigenous peoples have had to give up in order to win these sovereignty victories. By fighting European states on their own turf, they have had to accept some of the premises of that turf. As Biolsi notes, the law is "a fundamental constituting axis of modern social life – not just a political resource or an institution but a constituent of all social relations of domination."[15] One danger is, therefore, that native communities become vulnerable to legal setbacks even as they use legal strategies to resist in-corporation and global capitalism when they are available.[16]

While many of the examples of indigenous resistance cited so far have been focused on specific locations, recent decades have also witnessed the emergence of international networks that aim to support indigenous movements. NGOs like Cultural Survival, the International Work Group on Indigenous Affairs, the Center for World Indigenous Studies, and the United Nations Working Group on Indigenous Populations have played an important role in advocating on behalf of threatened indigenous communities.[17]

Meanwhile, the Zapatista movement has mounted an even more dramatic challenge to global capitalism. By openly rejecting conventional modernization and development projects, and seeking to maintain traditional ways of life, Zapatista communities aim to forge a new alternative. The high level of national and international support that has been given to the Zapatista struggle

---

[14] Mullis and Kamper (2000); Fenelon (2000).
[15] Biolsi (1995: 543).
[16] Here we must note an important difference between indigenous struggles in the "first" world and those in the "third world." The rule of law carries much more force in the first world, and so is a more useful tool there. This difference holds as a "rule of thumb," but finds exceptions in both directions.
[17] Wilmer (1993); Smith and Ward (2000).

shows that these indigenous efforts to bring into existence alternatives to capitalism resonate across many sectors of global civil society.[18]

Although there is immense diversity in the characteristics of indigenous groups, we maintain that they do share one thing in common: all these forms of social organization are fundamentally non-capitalist in nature. Moreover, although indigenous peoples have been forced to deal with waves of European expansion for centuries, many have resisted incorporation heroically. Many indigenous communities have succeeded, at least partially, in retaining political, social, and cultural autonomy. Native peoples therefore continue to form an important movement of resistance to global capitalism, and to the concepts of sovereignty embedded in the modern world-system.

Indigenous Challenges to Global Capitalism

The survival of indigenous groups poses a number of important questions. How can we explain this survival capacity? And, to what extent do indigenous groups pose a real challenge to capitalism?

In our conceptualization, indigenous groups draw strength from kinship and community solidarities that are distinctly non-capitalist in nature. Of course, when ties of kinship and community coincide with ways of making a living, they become extremely powerful in binding people together and in maintaining a sense of solidarity. This is precisely what happens within most indigenous communities. But, beneath these economic links are powerful communal ties that provide alternative sources of solidarity.

Even when members participate in the wider capitalist economy and its wage labor processes, indigenous people generally remain tied in important ways to their communities. Thus, it is no accident that the most successful indigenous groups are ones who have some degree of access to a sufficiently large land base. Survival is therefore intimately tied to protecting this access to local resources in the homeland. For this reason, tribal and indigenous identities often become powerfully linked to specific geographic places (Champagne 2003, 2005; McLeod 2001).

Land and water resources tend to have meanings that go far beyond the purely economic, and instead reflect complex social and cultural necessities within the communities. Note that here we are not asserting that indigenous

---

[18] Ross (1995); Katzenberger (1995); Collier (1999).

peoples have some inherent connection to the environment. Instead, we echo Polanyi's (1944) argument that, before the "Great Transformation" wrought by capitalism, people of all types had strong, non-monetary connections to the natural environment.

It is not that indigenous peoples were unable to understand private property or land boundaries and established monetary value. It is that they generally rejected those concepts as invalid because of their distinct material needs and value systems. That rejection can be found in Crazy Horse's declaration that "One does not sell the land which the people walk upon," as well as in the Zapatista's rejection of private ownership of plantations in Chiapas. Each of these traditions represents resistance of the highest order to capitalist types of globalization.

One consequence of the space-time compression (Harvey 1989) associated with increasing globalization, has been that pressures for change of identity have become more overt, explicit, and obvious. Not surprisingly, efforts to resist those homogenizing pressures become more overt as well. These clashes seem to be most extreme when the incorporated or encapsulated groups are, or recently were, organized according to the logic of a different mode of accumulation.

Because such groups are organized according to a different social logic, they can sometimes be more of a threat to the overall system than challengers who are more economically, politically, or militarily powerful. This is because they are proof that the logic of the dominant system is not "natural," "normal," "manifest," or "inevitable." In short, by their very continued existence, indigenous peoples are concrete proof that shouts of TINA (There Is No Alternative) are false.[19]

With the end of the cold war and the collapse of any sort of immediately viable socialist alternative to capitalism, these challenges have increased in salience. This, of course, makes their continuing survival all the more puzzling. If they offer such a threat to ideological hegemony of the current system, why have they not been summarily crushed? In part, the answer is that many have. But within capitalist culture's self-conception, wholesale slaughter of human beings for the "crime" of being different has become unacceptable. And, at other times, geopolitical considerations create limited protections for indigenous groups. For instance, the willingness of the Turkish Parliament

---

[19] See Bennholdt-Thomsen et al. (2001).

to grant some new rights to Kurds derived from Turkey's desire to join the EU. This is an example of how changing global climate can sometimes change the playing field in the struggle for indigenous rights.

Even when challengers use whatever they gain from "playing the capitalist game" (as with Native American gaming operations) to preserve their non-capitalist organization, they have not been perceived as a severe threat to the overall system. There are at least two aspects to this. First, they do not challenge the system in an attempt to replace or overthrow it. Rather, they seek to carve out a niche within it. Second, most are relatively small in demographic, political, and resource terms. Thus, the threats of their existence as alternatives to the dominant mode of organization are outweighed by the self-contradictions that would be made manifest by overt attempts to destroy them.

However, we should not lose sight of the very skillful efforts of indigenous leaders to play upon these contradictions to defend their niches within the world-system. Wilmer (1993) has observed that indigenous leaders have often drawn on European jurisprudence to assert their right to exist. Many indigenous leaders have pointed out that, if their sovereignty is summarily annihilated, then the basic tenants of the Treaty of Westphalia (1648) – and the protections it conferred to sovereign peoples in the modern inter-state system – is called into question. Clearly, the dilemmas posed by indigenous groups raise important questions about concepts of political sovereignty in the contemporary period.

Indigenous Challenges to Nation-State Sovereignty

In recent decades, a scholarly debate has emerged about the power and relevance of individual states in a system that is becoming increasingly globalized, and dominated by non-state actors like multi-national corporations. Sklair (2002), for instance, argues that a transnational capitalist class is emerging that is more powerful than political authorities in many regions of the world. He therefore faults those who continue to focus on the nation-state as the key unit of analysis when examining the capitalist world-economy. Wallerstein (2002), for his part, argues that global capitalism (and the transnational capitalist class) continues to rely on the military and political power wielded by the world's nation-states.

We take an intermediate position in this debate. We contend that the emerging transnational capitalist class simultaneously seeks to subvert and transcend the state in many ways, while also making use of state power when it serves its purposes. We therefore argue that the world is shifting away from the traditions forged in the Treaty of Westphalia, and toward a still-undefined new political order at the global level. These changes will require further modifications to the analysis of sovereignty.

We also contend that the efforts of indigenous groups to protect and enhance their autonomy pose additional challenges to classical understandings of sovereignty. These challenges from below will also play a significant role in creating a set of political rules. This is because most indigenous peoples represent an alternative to capitalist accumulation that poses a fundamental challenge to formal state sovereignty. Even as conflicts between states and transnational capitalist interests play themselves out at one level of the system, indigenous peoples will continue to resist and challenge at another.

Once again, it is instructive to see how these battles over sovereignty are played out in the very heart of the system. The United States government has developed a detailed set of treaties and regulations meant to bring order to the complex interactions that take place between the federal, state, and local governments – and the indigenous peoples who survived conquest with some degree of sovereignty intact. The Canadian government faces a similarly complex situation. Indeed, some analysts argue that the Canadian government has been more humane than that of the US, since Canadian authorities have recognized some sovereignty claims captured in the oral traditions of their "First Nations" while the US has been reticent to do so (Perry 1996).

As the state system moved throughout its violent growth and development, different kinds of treaties have been entered into by indigenous peoples.[20] Early treaties often favored native peoples, since native nations were quite strong vis-a-vis colonizers. During these early encounters in the United States, for example, indigenous peoples were generally able to win recognition of their tribal sovereignty within areas that had been conquered. Over time, though, indigenous peoples found it increasingly difficult to ensure that these treaties were closely followed. In fact, it became quite common for agents of nation-states to violate legal treaties. What emerged out of this long history in the United States, for instance, was a complex set of "dual sovereignty" relationships – where federal and state sovereignty reigned supreme, but contested arenas of tribal authority were also retained (Fenelon 2002). The newly developing nation-states of the western hemisphere, including the

---

[20] Deloria and Lytle (1984); Deloria and Wilkins (1999); Wilkins (2002).

United States, assumed they could extinguish these tribal claims to sovereignty at a later date.

However, that has not proven to be the case. In fact, from Canada, to the United States, to Mexico, and across other countries of the world, indigenous peoples have actually increased the scope of their own political sovereignty in recent decades. What has emerged is a complex, highly contested mix of styles of sovereignty. We review briefly some of the new kinds of sovereignty conflicts that have emerged in the western hemisphere – at the very heart of the modern inter-state system.[21]

During centuries of resistance, for instance, the Mohawk have fought to protect their autonomy against incursions from US and Canadian authorities. As a result of their persistent struggles, which erupted in armed conflict as recently as the 1990s, the Mohawk have won significant degrees of sovereignty in each country. Similarly, the Lakota (Sioux) have engaged in over two hundred years of struggle to protect their claims to sovereignty and control over land. Since the 1960s, activists have increasingly used old treaties as the basis for legal claims designed to reassert Lakota authority over lands and communities. The Puyallup provide another good example of how a tribe can be almost driven out of existence, but then succeed in reclaiming some degree of sovereignty. Other examples abound, from the Puyallup, to the Cherokee, to the Pequot, to the Yaqui, and beyond. In each case, tribes that were almost driven out of existence have succeeded in rallying themselves, and reclaiming some degree of sovereignty at the heart of the world-system in North America.

Further to the south, Mayan peoples in Chiapas, Mexico, have mounted armed and non-violent resistance to U.S.-led forms of globalization. The Zapatistas state that their struggle has been going on for "500 years," and that their target is transnational capitalism, hemispheric hegemony, and the repression of the peasant Indian. Clearly, in this case modern revolutionary forms of struggle have been linked with indigenous forms of resistance to create a very powerful, complex form of resistance to global capitalism and the power of the Mexican state.

Of course, we should not assume that there is an inevitable, natural link between revolutionary and indigenous struggles. The experience of the Miskito in Nicaragua shows that a revolutionary government may at times try to

---

[21] See Hall and Fenelon (2003, in press a, b) for a more detailed discussion of these kinds of cases.

impose its own political agenda on indigenous peoples. The Sandinistas were in part trying to counter Contra/US attempts to recruit Miskito people into counter-revolutionary activities. However, the Sandanista regime was also trying to impose stronger control over a people who had retained some degree of sovereignty within Nicaragua. This example demonstrates that political elites of almost any political orientation attempt to exercise their sovereignty over indigenous peoples within their borders.

One response on the part of indigenous peoples to threats from centers of political power is to organize, and attempt to seize control of that power through electoral means. This is exactly what has occurred with growing frequency in South America. Quechua people in Ecuador, for instance, have formed political organizations that have played central roles in the tumultuous political events of that country. Indigenous parties are also exerting an increasing power in Peru, Bolivia, Colombia, Venezuela, and even in Hawaii. Of course, there are dangers inherent in this electoral strategy. Political machinations can damage the image of indigenous leaders. Moreover, there is always the danger that, by partaking in conventional politics, indigenous peoples will subsumed into the general population and ways of conducting politics. Still, the growth of indigenous political parties across the western hemisphere is a dramatic illustration of the continuing survival and resilience of native peoples.

While achieving some degree of political protection and power is clearly important if indigenous peoples are to increase their sovereignty, there is another dynamic in operation that poses additional challenges. Across the world, commercial pressures to penetrate into indigenous regions in order to extract natural resources such as oil, gold, and other products are intensifying. Although indigenous peoples may have won political rights and may even be legally offered protection from incursions, these commercial forces can pose severe threats. The Yanomami of Venezuela, for instance, are witnessing growing trespassing into their legally-recognized reserves by gold prospectors and other outsiders. In some cases, development projects funded by organizations like the IMF and the World Bank intensify these incursions. Across the entire developing world, indigenous groups who have succeeded in winning some degree of political recognition are therefore facing a new, profound threat.

This brief review shows that political relationships between nation-states and indigenous peoples are growing increasingly complex in the western hemisphere. So, even in regions where the capitalist world-system has achieved quite deep penetration, indigenous peoples have succeeded in surviving and sometimes even enhancing their power. Much more research is needed to tease out the complex relations that exist between indigenous struggles for survival, nation-state reactions, and broader world-systemic dynamics. Still, it is clear that indigenous peoples have been mounting significant challenges to the political sovereignty of nation-states in recent decades. But, what are the prospects for these challenges in the post 9/11 era – when governments have even greater incentives to try to impose control over the peoples and resources that lie within their borders? This is the question we turn to in the conclusion of our chapter.

Prospects for Indigenous Sovereignty in the Twenty-First Century

Though subjected to centuries of colonization and oppression, indigenous peoples across the world have managed to persist as important, non-capitalist kinds of societies. But will indigenous peoples be able to continue to mount challenges to the dominant capitalist world-system? Might the resurgence of a US-defined "manifest destiny" that emphasizes national security, political control, and free markets, foreshadow a new period of attack on indigenous sovereignty and diversity across the world?

In providing provisional answers to this crucial question, we must first recognize that indigenous peoples have shown an amazing capacity to survive harsh processes of conquest and assimilation over the last five thousand years. Even after being subjected to systemic attacks, indigenous peoples still number some 350 millions – which is approximately 5 per cent of the world's population.[22] And within indigenous communities we can find an impressive array of alternatives to capitalism. Indeed, it could be argued that the alternatives that exist within native lands are more diverse and innovative than the oppositional projects that have been constructed by citizens who are fully assimilated into the capitalist world-system. Rather than proposing the construction of a "kinder, gentler" form of capitalism or consumer society, indigenous peoples manifest a panoply of fundamentally different kinds of alternatives.

---

[22] This information is drawn from various U.N. websites. Other sources are: Wilmer 1993; Smith and Ward 2000; Bodley 2003.

We have already described some of the examples of indigenous resistance that have taken place in North America – where the capitalist system has had an opportunity to deeply penetrate societies. In other regions of the world, where the process of incorporation is still not complete, there are also fertile opportunities for indigenous resistance. From the Warli peoples of India, to the Kurds, to the Maori, the Iban, the Pashtun, and many others, indigenous peoples across the world are struggling to protect their unique identities, cultures, and autonomy. Many more studies are needed to delineate the entire range of alternatives and resistances that indigenous peoples present. Our point here is that these resistances are occurring in all regions of the world.

It is also reasonable to expect that, to the degree that indigenous peoples do succeed in resisting capitalism, they will call down stronger attempts to change or destroy them. The most successful tactics of assimilation, however, are not likely to be frontal attacks, but more invidious erosions via media exposure, increasing dependence on the products of capitalism, and incremental increases in participation in the global economy.

This is why the experience of the Zapatistas may be so prophetic. It is addressing such forces directly. Thus far, it has succeeded in gaining converts and fellow travelers among the middle classes of the world, and linking with other anti-globalization forces. Indeed, the Zapatistas may be moving into a position of global leadership in resisting globalization. The slogan, "We are all Indians of the World" seeks to build solidarity with others on the basis of recognition that all individuals are being crushed by global capitalism. Such attempts at broad solidarity are common among indigenous movements.[23]

Whether this, or any other movement, will succeed remains unknown. If one takes a short-run view, over the era of capitalist domination of the last few centuries, evidence would suggest capitalism will win in the end. If, however, one takes a very long run view, many types of indigenous organizations have withstood assaults of states, not for centuries, but millennia. Hence, the evidence would suggest indigenous peoples will survive. If one looks further into the rise of the capitalist world-system, one notes capitalism came to dominate from little pockets scattered here and there for millennia, and thus recognizes that modern capitalism is an amalgam of older forms

---

[23] For instance, the lead singer Klee Benally of Blackfire introduces their set with a statement that all movements, anti-globalization, anti-sexist, anti-racist, anti-homophobic are all the same movement as their movement for survival (Blackfire 2001).

and newer forms (Chase-Dunn and Hall 1997), then one might expect that whatever the world-system transforms into will be built on the various models that already exist. And here, clearly, indigenous peoples represent the widest range of alternatives and continuously adapting forms from which to build a more inclusive new world.

With these broad points in mind, we can now turn to the issue of the impacts of the 9/11 attacks and the "war on terrorism." The preceding analysis and discussion suggests that to ask about the impacts of these events is to ask the wrong question. Why should such events, spectacular though they have been, impact processes of resistance that have been going on for millennia? At most we would expect slight perturbations in a trajectory of resistance, along the lines of those documented by Podobnik (this volume). Our argument follows that of Dunaway (2003a) and Wallerstein (2003), who claim that the 9/11 attacks and subsequent wars are part and parcel of the normal processes of capitalist dynamics. As Clark (2002) argues, the intensification, the speeding up, the increasing interconnectedness of global capitalism makes a large variety of "normal accidents" more, not less, likely.

Precisely because they so often try to exist outside the system, many indigenous groups may be better insulated from such "normal accidents" than members of societies that are fully integrated into the capitalist world-system. Furthermore, as ethnic conflict has become more costly to the system (Dunaway 2003b), there may well be less pressure to integrate indigenous peoples more fully. Indeed, to the degree that global elites increasingly attend to the rising risks in the centers of power, they may pay even less attention to indigenous peoples. If so, the impact of 9/11 and other such recent events may actually enhance the probability of their continued survival.

Yet, if indigenous peoples associate themselves with anti-globalization or fundamentalist movements, they do run the risk of being accused of being terrorists. They also increase the likelihood that the "war on terror" will be used in part to force greater indigenous assimilation into global culture. Still, it is our opinion that 9/11 is at best a blip on the radar in the long history of these indigenous struggles, and is not necessarily a marker of any sort of significant change.

Indigenous peoples across the world have carried out impressive struggles for survival and autonomy for a very long time. In the course of their campaigns, indigenous communities have demonstrated that human beings do have the capacity to resist in the face of even the most brutal processes of incorporation in the capitalist world-system. They have also created many alternative forms of social organization, which shows that global capitalism is not a natural or inevitable form of human interactions. Through their persistent and often successful struggles, indigenous peoples offer everyone hope that the dominant system can be resisted, and perhaps ultimately transformed into a more humane and diverse form of global society.

Robert J.S. Ross

From Anti-Sweatshop, to Global Justice, to Anti-War: Student Participation in Globalization Protests

Introduction

In January 1999, a new student movement announced itself on the campuses of American universities. The movement began a campaign for a "sweat free campus" in dramatic fashion, by occupying administration buildings on seven university campuses across the country. In each case, the students' demands were focused on labor exploitation in the apparel industry. In the intervening years, the anti-sweatshop movement has joined with other groups to form a global justice and anti-war movement. Overall, the anti-sweatshop movement has emerged as an enduring and important participant in globalization protests in the current era.

In this chapter, I analyze the anti-sweatshop movement's evolution with two key goals in mind. First, I compare it to its nearest historic analogue, the 1960s organization Students for a Democratic Society (SDS). The second axis of this analysis is an inquiry into the ways in which the growth of global capitalism and some of its technological media have affected the evolution of the movement.

The Formation of USAS

The campus-based anti-sweatshop campaign has its clearest origins in policies undertaken by the AFL-CIO after 1995. Under the presidency of John Sweeney, new efforts were undertaken to revive organizing activity after a long period of union decline. First, the AFL-CIO created an Organizing Institute (OI) to train new organizers. This institute then engaged in an aggressive outreach effort, which included recruitment among college students and recent graduates. The OI also initiated a program called Union Summer. Echoing the Mississippi Freedom Summer of 1964, Union Summer encouraged young adults to "try out" the labor movement by enrolling in a variety of summer internships (Weisbrot 1990).

In the summer of 1997, a group of Union Summer interns at the offices of the former International Ladies' Garment Workers Union (ILGWU) in New York[1] began to develop the idea of a "sweat free campus." Ginny Coughlin, a supervisor with experience in the Democratic Socialists of America (DSA), helped them elaborate the idea. One of these interns was Tico Almeida, a student at Duke University (Ginny Coughlin 2002). Almeida would become a central figure in the anti-sweatshop movement over the coming years.

The campaign for sweat free campuses decided to begin by targeting the large market of school-insignia clothing that exists in the United States. In this market, a university licenses a private company to use its logo and name on apparel. In turn, the company pays the school a fee for the right to print the logos. About 180 of the largest schools use the Collegiate Licensing Company (CLC) to manage their licensing deals.

In response to an early wave of protests, in 1998 the CLC adopted its own Code of Conduct that paralleled the code adopted by the broader Fair Labor Association was supposed to ease labor problems. However, the industry-sponsored code proved to be inadequate, and students continued to target schools that made use of CLC services.

One of the early protests was undertaken by Tico Almeida and other students at Duke University. The students contacted their President, and urged that the school adopt a more stringent Code of Conduct that would govern licensees producing Duke logo clothing.[2] The Duke administration did adopt

---

[1] Now the headquarters of the merged UNITE/HERE including the ILGWU and the Amalgamated Clothing and Textile Workers Union (ACTWU) and The Hotel Employees & Restaurant Employees Union.

[2] The general idea was based on Notre Dame's pioneering 1996 code – a product of Jesuit social conscience, not a social movement outside of usual channels.

a new code. But, as it turned out, the Duke Administration's agreement did not require companies to provide a complete list of the factories used by contractors – which was a fatal flaw in the eyes of the students.

When a university grants a license to a firm, that firm usually contracts with other factories to manufacture the garments. A staggering number of distinct factories, each with their own labor conditions, can therefore be involved in the apparel commodity chain.[3] The students demanded that companies provide a complete list of the factories involved, but in general these requests were rejected by the companies. The Duke students therefore held a sit-in in January 1999, which convinced the administration to adopt a full disclosure policy. At the same time, a separate group of students at the University of North Carolina demanded that a stricter code of conduct be applied to a new contract that Nike was negotiating with their school (Traub-Werner 1999).

While students on these two campuses were working on their local campaigns, organizers were linking student groups across many campuses. In the summer of 1998 students from 30 campuses met in New York to form "an informal but cohesive international coalition of campuses and individual students working on anti-sweatshop and Code of Conduct campaigns."[4] By early 1999, the organization United Students Against Sweatshops (USAS) had been formed. Within a short time, groups on about 50 campuses across the country were working under this umbrella organization. Groups loosely affiliated with USAS held sit-ins on at least seven campuses, and had held rallies demanding stricter codes of conduct at many other locations. In the course of 1999, then, a new activist movement was clearly taking shape on American campuses.

USAS continued to link up with new campus groups throughout the next academic year. And it also added a new dimension to its activity. Reacting to union criticism of industry-created codes of conduct, a student group at Brown University devised an alternative plan for insuring University licensed apparel would be "sweat free".

Industry-sponsored codes of conduct had stemmed from a Clinton Administration initiative to bring the "stakeholders" – firms, unions and human

---

[3] There are almost 3000 entries in the University of Michigan database of factory locations for calendar year 2002; of these my estimate is that there are about 2000 discrete factories that produce everything from glasses to coolers to t-shirts to t-shirt printing. (Workers Rights Consortium factory database:http://workersrights.org/fdd.asp).
[4] USAS (2002).

rights groups, and consumers – together to develop an industry-wide code that would enable consumers to choose "sweat free" clothing. The result was the Fair Labor Association (FLA), which made some progress in defining what a "fair labor" garment meant.[5] However, many union and student groups came to believe that the FLA codes had important flaws. They required that firms pay official minimum wages rather than living wages; they did not call for the full disclosure of locations; the monitoring protocol called for sampling only 10% of contractor locations per year; and the corporations were initially allowed to hire their own monitors.[6] Given these important limitations, the student coalition decided to create an alternative organization that would certify sweat free clothing using stricter standards.

The alternative organization came to be called the Worker Rights Consortium. The WRC differs in important ways from the FLA. In contrast to the FLA, for instance, the WRC board has no corporate members. Moreover, it hires independent labor and human rights organizations to obtain information from workers about factory conditions. And the codes of conduct that its university members impose on licensees are stronger. Once in existence, the student organizations began demanding that their campuses join the WRC rather than the FLA. And, against many predictions, USAS was successful in getting over 50 universities and colleges to join the WRC within the first two years of its existence. By May 2002, the 100th institution had joined the WRC; by early 2005 there were 134.

Although this represents an important achievement on campuses, the college apparel market is only about 1–2% of the entire clothing market in the United States. It is still unclear, therefore, how much of an impact the student-led movement is having on the broader industry.

It may be possible that universities can be used as bridgeheads for prompting wider change. The factories that perform college logo work also generally perform other work. So, if they can be pressured to change the ways they produce college clothing, it could carry over into their non-college production as well. It appears that this has already occurred in certain cases. For example, a cap factory in the Dominican Republic that was making college apparel agreed, under pressure from the WRC, to recognize its workers' union. Because the factory also produced items for Nike, Reebok, and other com-

---

[5] The original conference and working group was called, in 1996, the Apparel Industry Partnership (AIP). For a history see Ross (2004).
[6] UNITE 1998; USAS 1999.

panies, this shift toward unionized labor had a larger impact on the industry (Ross 2004).

Public opinion surveys indicate that a substantial majority of U.S. consumers is willing to pay slightly more for apparel they are certain is "sweat-free."[7] This suggests that the "ethical" market is large enough to sustain some sizeable enterprises. This was the logic behind SWEATX, a new unionized t-shirt maker, funded by "Ben" of Ben and Jerry's famous ice cream, and an East coast version, No Sweat Apparel, made by Bienestar International.[8]

The creation and growth of the WRC are major victories for the new student movement. In fact, by the summer of 2003, USAS claimed over 200 campus groups. This rate of growth is greater than that achieved by Students for a Democratic Society prior to 1965, or that achieved by northern support groups for the southern civil rights movement in the early 1960s. The comparison provides fascinating insight to the perennial question of historical analysis: what is the same, what is different, and why?

A Comparison of SDS and USAS

SDS and USAS can be compared along a number of dimensions. In what follows, I will compare and contrast the demographic backgrounds of activists in each group, how each group spread geographically, and the different kinds of tactics and ideologies that were used by each organization.[9]

Tom Hayden, first President of Students for a Democratic Society, wrote in the Port Huron Statement that "We are people of this generation bred in at least modest affluence, housed in the universities, looking uncomfortably to the worlds we inherit." Initially, most SDS participants came from upper middle class homes.[10] By 1967, however, the movement had incorporated students of working class and lower white-collar families. Institutionally,

---

[7] Marymount (1999); Pollin et al. (2001); Program on International Policy Attitudes (2000).

[8] In May 2004, SweatX folded. No Sweat apparel is still in business as is another "sweatshop free local (LA) producer, American Apparel. Relatively high wage, American Apparel is nevertheless nonunion (Strasburg 2004; Slater 2004).

[9] The analysis of USAS is based on extensive interviews with movement leaders, and on participant observation work carried out by the author. Information about SDS comes from my personal involvement in the organization, as well as from academic research.

[10] See Flacks (1967, 1971) and Mankoff and Flacks (1971) for more detailed information.

the movement began at exclusive or elite private colleges and flagship state universities like Berkeley, Wisconsin and Michigan; it later spread to less elite private and public colleges.

Research on the backgrounds of student activists in the 1960s has shown that organization leaders tended to come from families which were ideologically progressive and egalitarian. Activists reported more equal relations between their mothers and fathers, and higher levels of education among their mothers, than did non-activists.[11]

This kind of research into today's campus movement has just begun. Nevertheless, it seems that the USAS leadership tends to come from middle or upper middle class, professional families. One study of anti sweatshop activists, for instance, finds that they are twice as likely to come from high income households as are the universe of college freshman (Elliot and Freeman 2000).

Meanwhile, there are interesting differences in the geographic diffusion patterns of SDS and USAS. The older movement coalesced within more selective elite institutions, and then moved outward into public universities. This diffusion process accelerated after SDS was "discovered" by the national press in 1965, when the organization carried out the March on Washington to End the War in Vietnam. By the late 1960s, even many community colleges had chapters of SDS or similar groups.

The diffusion of the contemporary USAS, meanwhile, has been much more rapid.[12] The first wave of sit-ins, in 1999, was at relatively "elite" or flagship state universities. By spring 2000, though, sit-ins were occurring in many different kinds of institutions of higher learning. Chapters in schools in Alabama, Arkansas, Georgia, and South Carolina became active relatively quickly, for instance. Overall, the WRC had chapters on over 100 institutions of higher education by 2003. USAS has clearly spread to non-elite institutions much faster than did SDS. In fact, the USAS rapid evolution approximates that achieved by student chapters of civil rights organizations, which spread the sit-ins and lunch counter boycotts around the south within weeks. It also compares to the tremendous growth of SDS after the March on Washington of April 1965.

---

[11] Flacks (1971).

[12] I have supplemented work first done by Aaron Kreider, then an undergraduate at Notre Dame University, who summarized the institutional rankings of campuses where major USAS actions occurred between 1999 and 2000 (Kreider 2000, 2002).

A similarity between SDS and USAS is the use of the sit-in to attempt to win change. USAS uses sit-ins to pressure universities to adopt codes of conduct and/or to affiliate with the WRC; SDS used sit-ins to attempt to force administrations to withhold grades from the Selective Service system (which used them to determine student deferments for the draft during the Vietnam War) and in other local disputes.

When McAdam (1982) mapped the Southern student civil rights sit-ins of 1960, he found that sit-ins spread from place to place through chains of physical proximity. No similar mapping study has been done of SDS, but my personal observation of chapter growth is similar. In each region, locally or self-designated "travelers" would set out to organize SDS chapters within driving distance from the base campus or city.

Among activists and observers today there is universal agreement that e-mail, the internet, and cheaper long distance phone service has changed the way ideas and movements spread from person to person. This ease of communication means that new movements among those "wired" up spread with much less physical proximity than in earlier periods.

The movements are quite similar in their focus on direct action, and rejection of relying on electoral approaches to achieving social change. Indeed, each organization has gone through something of a process of ideological radicalization. At the outset of the civil rights movement, the emerging student movement's demands were for relatively modest reforms. But SDS began broadening the scope of movement critique, projecting a radical democratic critique and vision. By 1969, some SDS student leaders thought that campus issues were more or less irrelevant, and they became focused on the creation of "revolutionary consciousness" in broader arenas. We can observe a similar evolution in some campus activists away from focus on the sweatshop issue, and towards broader issues in the world-economy. While not yet creating the kind of hyper-revolutionary rhetoric found in organizations like the Weather Underground in the 1960s, there is nevertheless something of a similar dynamic in motion today. In the contemporary period, we see an evolution from support for sit-ins, to a general "tolerance" of street vandalism against symbols of neo-liberalism.

We need to be careful when summarizing the ideological characteristics of such broad movements, of course. Members of SDS adopted a great variety of stances, from mainstream liberalism, to anarchism, to communism, radical Christianity, and others.

By 1968, most new leftists who were politically active were more or less anti-capitalist and radically democratic. And, by that time, many SDSers' view of appropriate tactics became more militant.

The leaders of today's anti-sweatshop movement are more or less explicitly anti-capitalist, and certainly "anti-corporate' in sentiment.[13] Many also incorporate other forms of social critique into their activism as well. Here, for instance, is an opening paragraph from a Mission Statement from a local global action network: "The people of WoGAN are feminist, partner preference supportive, anti-imperialist, anti-classist, anti-capitalist, anti-racist as well as being respectful toward all forms of life, all religions and the diversity of human experience. We believe that all should have equal access and equal voice in the global community. We view direct action as a viable method of decentralizing control and establishing autonomy" (WoGan website). In sum, the current cohort of young activists, and their political evolution, is, for better and for worse, not so different from the radicals of SDS.

The biggest difference between today's activists and those of the 1960s is the current cohort's positive relation to the labor movement and to class issues. SDS activists were generally critical of the labor movement and invested in (residential) community issues.[14] The new movements of the 1990s are more influenced by reformers within the AFL-CIO. In my view, this recent student-labor alliance is traceable to the emergence of global capitalism.

Many 1960s activists did not include the mass of blue-collar workers as a focus of concern or sympathy. By the year 2000 though, union density in the private sector was one third of what it was in the 1960s. This reversal of fortune of the labor movement has provoked a change in attitude of union leaders toward creating coalitions with students. The development of Jobs with Justice metropolitan areas coalitions is an example: most of these welcome student allies and religious and other community linkages. The pressures of the last twenty years have seen a revival, in some places, of social movement unionism. And some unions have put their money where their rhetoric is. Indeed, the AFL-CIO has given major contributions to USAS.[15]

---

[13] The vast majority of the USAS activists I interviewed in the late 1990s said that they were socialists, or sympathetic to a socialist vision of society. However, they did not think that they could communicate this vision to their peers or to other Americans using socialist terminology.

[14] It is important not to over-state the student/labor divide in the 1960s. Note that the SDS Port Huron Statement was written at a Michigan AFL-CIO summer camp. Many of the leading figures at Port Huron came from union homes.

[15] Voss and Sherman (2000); Featherstone (2002).

There are also important differences between the organizational forms adopted by current students and those from the 1960s. SDS had a rather conventional organizational structure. Chapters were entitled to certain numbers of votes at conventions, and conventions then elected representative bodies. Meetings ranged from highly informal to highly parliamentary – depending and size and the level of internal contention.[16] The preferred use of consensus decision-making was restricted to small groups and a limited period of time.

By contrast, groups in the new global justice movement have elaborately formalized consensus decision-making procedures. They eschew representative forms almost entirely. In this, USAS will probably rediscover the old problems of such open and unformed organizations. For instance, they are vulnerable to indecision and to factional intrusion by more disciplined outsiders. Indeed, by 2002–2003 the new antiwar movement, of which USAS was but one part, was confronted with the fact that an extremely small, sectarian group – the Workers World Party – had seized control of the demonstration-calling apparatus (the ANSWER coalition) that had sponsored the biggest antiwar marches.

One very strong difference between the internal workings of USAS and SDS is the sophistication of USAS training in and understanding of group process. USAS meetings are characterized by teaching and the use of fairly sophisticated techniques of group discussion and leadership. Participatory observation of USAS meetings demonstrated their painstaking efforts to include all participants in discussion, and active care to insure that women were selected as discussion leaders or representatives and spokespersons.

Looking beyond the orbit of USAS, to the broader global justice movement, a more ideological commitment to anarchism is gaining ideological hegemony. For instance organizers of the Boston Social Forum attempted to put into practice new anarchists organizational models. The new activists seem to be moving from anti-corporate, to anti-capitalist, and perhaps to radically localist visions.

---

[16] These observations are based on widespread and long-term personal observation. See also Rothstein (1989).

The Impact of 9/11 on Contemporary Student Activism

Most mainstream Americans feel personally threatened and even angry about the attack of September 11, 2001.[17] For some, these sentiments translated into strong support for the Bush Administration, and its bellicose reactions. But for those on the left, the attacks spurred a number of different responses.

On the one hand, many moderates tried to investigate the conditions that produced the terrorist attacks. It was widely noted that Middle Eastern societies are dominated by undemocratic regimes. And the long history of US interventionism in the region was argued to have fostered resentment – especially since American administrations often supported regimes that brutalized dissidents. The result was a somewhat understandable animosity toward the United States, it was often argued.

The journalist Robert Fisk, who covered the war in Afghanistan, expressed this kind of perspective in particularly poignant terms. Just after he was attacked by a mob of Afghan refugees, he wrote: "If I was an Afghan refugee in Kila Abdullah, I would have done just what they did. I would have attacked Robert Fisk. Or any other Westerner I could find" (Fisk 2001).

This kind of stance often led to the argument that the September 11 attacks were in some sense "just deserts." Some student activists stated that US policy "deserved" the anger of the "wretched of the earth." In some ways, these radical arguments came close to echoing the position developed by the Weather Underground thirty years earlier – which argued that violent attacks from the third world needed to be carried out in centers of global power. And, just as in the late 1960s, the possibility emerged that damaging splits in the left would emerge over these kinds of arguments.

However, there is evidence to suggest that disagreements over the 9/11 attacks, and the subsequent military conflicts, are not splintering the critics of corporate globalization. For instance, no serious ideological divide has emerged between student and labor groups. This is largely because most students and labor activists share a surprisingly similar view on recent conflict. On the one hand, USAS has openly stated its opposition to the War in Iraq – as have most student organizations across the country. At the same time, perhaps more surprisingly, labor leaders have adopted a modestly anti-war position themselves.

---

[17] Institute for Social Research (2001).

As the Bush and Blair governments moved toward war, for example, the AFL-CIO joined the British Trades Union Congress to urge caution. "The goal of our policy," they wrote, "should be to take every possible step to achieve the legitimate ends of disarming Iraq without recourse to war . . ." (Monks and Sweeney 2003). In an even more strongly worded statement published soon after, the AFL-CIO Executive Committee asserted that "the President has not fulfilled his responsibility to make a compelling and coherent explanation to the American people and the world about the need for military action against Iraq at this time" (AFL-CIO 2003).

As further indication that students and labor unions are still actively collaborating, joint student/labor internships and organizing workshops continue to be offered by the AFL-CIO and USAS through the summer of 2005. Meanwhile, renewed efforts are underway to carry out anti-sweat shop campaigns on many campuses across North America.

While processes of radicalization occasionally took students into sectarian and isolating forms of activism in the 1960s, this dynamic does not seem to be as powerful in the current period. There certainly are extremely radical pockets of students that take part in current protests, often under anarchist banners. However, the vast majority of the anti-sweat shop activists continue doggedly forward in efforts to publicize labor abuses across the world. In early 2005, major actors in the sweat free campaign decided to turn its "sweat free" focus towards a union preference strategy. In the meantime, the broader radical global justice movement was gearing up for a campaign against the new free trade agreements – and agenda shared with labor. Everything suggests, therefore, that students are still very active participants in the anti-corporate and anti-war mobilizations even as its anti-sweatshop wing maintains ties to the labor movement.

Kenneth Gould, Tammy Lewis, and J. Timmons Roberts

Blue-Green Coalitions: Constraints and Possibilities in the Post 9/11 Political Environment

Introduction

During a key moment of the 1999 WTO protest in Seattle, as police amassed around a group of demonstrators, an event of huge symbolic importance occurred. A cluster of young environmentalists, dressed in sea turtle costumes, looked up to find that a group of truck drivers from the Teamsters Union had moved in to offer their protection. "Turtles love Teamsters," said one young environmentalist. "Teamsters love Turtles," responded a tough truck driver. It appeared, to those on the scene and to later commentators, that an alliance of historic importance was cemented on the streets of Seattle. Environmentalists and union workers had finally joined together to resist the agenda being pushed forward by institutions like the World Trade Organization.

Since 1999, environmentalists and workers have come to make up two of the largest contingents of the emerging movement against corporate-led globalization. Each group is driven by similar exigencies. Environmentalists fear that a "race to the bottom" is underway, as regulations that were developed over decades are overturned by international financial institutions. Labor unions fear that a massive flow of jobs to overseas sites will occur, and that wages and working conditions will plummet on a global level. Driven by a common antagonism toward the

World Trade Organization, environmentalists and workers therefore found it easy to join together in a spontaneous alliance. Indeed, analysts began to predict that, on the basis of this "Blue/Green Coalition," a serious challenge to the neo-liberal agenda could be mounted in North America and across the world.

Eighteen months later, though, the picture had dramatically shifted. The coalition became deeply divided over energy policy changes proposed by Vice-President Dick Cheney. Cheney brought union leaders to the White House to gain their support for drilling in the Artic National Wildlife Refuge, and for building thousands of new power plants. Unions were also encouraged to support relaxations in fuel-efficiency standards. And, finally, the Bush administration wanted support from labor in a campaign to oppose the Kyoto Treaty on global warming. On all four cases, labor sided with the administration and against their environmentalist counterparts.

Only a few years after the Seattle protests, the environment/labor coalition that had been forged in the United States has been badly damaged. The tenuousness of this coalition in North America suggests that it may be hard to sustain such alliances over the long term, and in other regions of the world. Clearly, a careful analysis of the evolution and current status of the environment/labor coalition is needed.

The Seattle Coalition: Marriage of Convenience or One Night Stand?

Despite the claims of media commentators and some activists, the WTO protests in Seattle in November of 1999 were not the result of a close collaboration between the major mainstream environmental organizations and organized labor. In fact, the level of actual direct working relations between these two segments of a much larger "coalition" was quite minimal.

The protest actions that received the most media attention were those organized through the Direct Action Network (DAN). DAN orchestrated the non-violent direct actions that included hard and soft lock downs at key intersections and the blockading of the convention center where the meetings of the WTO were to be held.[1] Those participating in the DAN direct actions, non-violence

---

[1] A "soft" lock down involves a symbolic connecting of protesters to each other and/or inanimate objects, usually through linking arms or string in conducting civil disobedience blockades of intersections and entrances. A "hard" lock down employs

trainings, and spokescouncil meetings represented a variety of organizations and interests – few of which were affiliated with organized labor or mainstream environmental organizations.[2] Instead, they represented smaller groups that focused on sweatshops, poverty in the global south, corporate power, human rights, indigenous rights, and a variety of anti-capitalist issues. While many of those participants would have called themselves environmentalists, and some of them were union members, they did not act directly in the name of those larger organizations (Danaher and Burbach 2000).

Meanwhile, there was a large organized labor presence at the protests in Seattle. Indeed, labor organizations provided the bulk of the funding for the protests, and some of the most disruptive actions were undertaken by unions. For instance, the ILWU called a shutdown of the ports on the entire west coast. It is important to note, however, that unions organized their own actions and marches, with little direct consultation or coordination with DAN or other activist groups. Meanwhile, the union rhetoric in Seattle focused on issues like wages, job losses, and sweatshop conditions. Rhetorical nods were occasionally made to the environment, but such issues never appeared as a high priority in union protests.

Workers did participate in at least one symbolic sit-down protest with DAN direct action protestors. But most of the joint demonstrating that occurred between workers, environmentalists, and others occurred spontaneously, in the midst of the chaos that ensued when the police rioted and demonstrators found themselves turning to each other for support. The real meeting of organized labor and other protesters only occurred when the labor and DAN marches were both violently attacked by the police. The convergence of marches did require some minimal coordination between environmental organizations and unions, but that relationship was mediated through DAN.

On the environmental side, the only highly visible mainstream group was Greenpeace. The turtle-costumed activists were organized by the Animal Welfare Institute and the Sea Turtle Restoration Project. Greenpeace has long been known as the odd member of the "Big 10" environmental organizations, given its use of non-violent direct action tactics and its critical focus on the

locks and chains, often with devices to prevent easy cutting by authorities, thus making such civil disobedience blockades more difficult to break up.
[2] A spokescouncil is a decision-making structure through which various groups coordinate actions and generate consensus. Protesters send delegates to the meetings to represent the consensus reached by their groups and organizations. This structure is intended to avoid the emergence of hierarchical decision-making structures.

policies of international financial institutions. So, it is no surprise that this organization was a key participant in the Seattle protests. Meanwhile, mainstream environmental groups were latecomers to the anti-corporate globalization campaign. Moreover, direct contact between mainstream environmental organizations and organized labor was minimal during the Seattle actions. The rhetoric of the environmental groups in Seattle was focused on issues of logging, endangered species, and genetically modified organisms, with only passing nods to labor and indigenous rights issues.

At no time did a unified rhetoric connecting labor and environment emerge from either camp in Seattle. What is clear from a review of the protests is that organized labor and mainstream environmental organizations protested the same institution, at the same meetings, but for different reasons. Both camps participated to some extent in the larger DAN coalition, but the bulk of the direct action protesters were affiliated with neither organized labor nor the mainstream environmental organizations. Claims about an emerging blue-green coalition were therefore based on the fact that both groups simultaneously, and with some minimal coordination, protested the same institution and set of policies. The fact that each camp articulated similar critiques of neoliberalism also tended to give the impression of unification.

All of these convergences were important, of course, and they signal the potential for a unified opposition and an even more ambitious unifying ideology. However, Seattle was not a reliable indicator that a blue-green coalition existed, nor that such a coalition would be sustainable over the long term. The Seattle protests against the WTO simply represented the finding of some common ground between organization that had been pitted against each other by corporations and the state for three decades (Kazis and Grossman 1991). At best, it was a marriage of convenience that could be developed into a lasting, mutually supportive relationship. At worst, it was a one-night stand unlikely to be repeated until blues and greens met again on the streets of Cancun, Mexico and Miami, Florida.

There have been enduring conflicts between labor and environmentalist groups. Although there are variations between various wings of each movement, there are some broad similarities in the underlying agendas pursued by each. For instance, unions tend to prioritize job growth and economic expansions. Environmentalists, on the other hand, argue that economic expansion threatens the sustainability of life on the planet, and that development projects need to be entirely rethought. In short, there are important potential conflicts in the long-range objectives of workers and environmentalists.

Contributing to this divide between greens and blues is the impact of the September 11, 2001, terrorist attacks. The events of 9/11 had a rather immediate impact on the US wing of the anti-corporate globalization movement, within which the new blue-green coalition was growing. On the day of the attacks, some members of Congress speculated that anti-corporate globalization activists might be responsible for the attack on the World Trade Center. While such speculation was quickly put to rest, it did become clear that there was rising hostility to radical forms of domestic dissent in the wake of the attacks (LeClerc and Gould 2003).

Organizations such as Mobilization for Global Justice, which had coordinated some mass protests, curtailed demonstrations. When protest reemerged at the World Economic Forum in New York, for instance, demonstrators were encouraged to obey laws and moderate their actions. Later protests at the IMF/WB meetings in Washington DC were similarly subdued.

The post-9/11 invasion of Iraq then drew energy away from the anti-corporate globalization movement, which further reduced the size and impact of globalization protests in the US. On the other hand, it is possible to identify some continuing efforts to strengthen the labor/environment coalition in the US and beyond. Under the leadership of John Sweeney of the AFL-CIO, there is a renewed effort being undertaken to recruit new members, foster a new form of social movement unionism, and fortify alliances with other groups. Efforts are also underway to foster international union links, such as that between the Sindicato de Petroleiros and Quimicos in Brazil and the PACE union in the US.

Within the United States, there is some evidence that grassroots groups engaged in environmental justice work are uniting environmentalists and labor activists in certain areas. But, at the level of national organizations, links between American environmental and union groups are still tenuous. Moreover, there is little evidence that enduring labor-environmental linkages are being created on the international level. This is unfortunate, since we believe that these international links are the key to supporting a longer-term "Seattle Coalition."

In what follows, we will argue that it is crucial to evaluate the interactions of environmental and labor groups at local, national, and international levels. Each level presents very different opportunities and pitfalls. In subsequent sections, we focus on key problems facing the blue-green coalition at these distinct levels of interaction. But first, let us review in some more detail the history of environmental and labor interactions in the United States.

Historical Roots of the Blue/Green Coalition[3]

While the labor movement has long delved into environmental concerns in the United States, there is little evidence that the mainstream environmental movement directly addressed labor concerns prior to 1999. Of course, there are many distinct streams of environmentalism in the U.S., from upper class preservation organizations, to groups that focus on health and safety concerns, to more radical forestry activist groups. Each form of environmentalism has produced unique obstacles and opportunities for creating blue-green coalitions. A brief examination of these divergent environmental histories can help illuminate the origin of current conflicts between potentially powerful coalition partners.

Up until the mid-1800s, the environment did not exist as an issue on the American political agenda. But, at the end of the nineteenth century, concerns began to grow about the long-term availability of natural resources that were crucial to future industrial expansion. As a result, some upper class citizens began to promote a mild form of conservationism that was aimed at protecting the capacity for continued economic growth.[4]

Other economically privileged groups also became concerned about environmental degradation at the turn of the century. Increased industrial pollution began to degrade many ecosystems, which hurt fishing and hunting activities. Preservationist groups therefore formed to protect specific areas for elite recreation. But these wealthy preservationists often sought to exclude poor and non-white citizens, which helped generate conflict between social classes around preservation issues (Dowie 1995).

At much the same time, an urban-based public health movement emerged to respond to the pollution problems being generated by industries in cities. Interestingly, this branch of American environmentalism was led primarily by women (Foster 1999). Its public health concerns were integrated into a larger agenda that aimed to improve the living conditions of workers and the unemployed. The demands of these activists would shortly be echoed by organized labor, in an early convergence between environmentalists and workers.

---

[3] The authors gratefully acknowledge the assistance of Andrew D. Van Alstyne in helping to frame the historical context of the movements.
[4] Schnaiberg (1980); Schnaiberg and Gould (2000).

Campaigns demanding improved working conditions and cleaner forms of production were fiercely opposed by corporate leaders, many of whom were at the same time taking advantage of the recreation opportunities established by preservationists. Still, unions were eventually able to demand that regulations be imposed to curb the most severe forms of industrial pollution. For instance, steelworkers demanded an investigation of deadly air inversions in 1948, while the United Auto Workers prioritized worker health issues prior to World War II. By the 1970s, labor unions were consistently placing environmental and health issues on the negotiating agenda across a wide range of industries.

Although there seemed to be a strong link between labor and environmental agendas, this convergence proved to be vulnerable to new changes that swept through the US from the 1960s on. The phenomenon of de-industrialization began to assail key centers of union strength, as companies increasingly relocated manufacturing facilities overseas. This process of relocation started to occur just as stronger environmental regulations were signed into law in the 1970s. As a result, industrial leaders and their allies were able to argue that job losses were being created by environmental regulations. Even though little empirical evidence suggests there is a connection between relocation and stricter environmental regulations, the argument was effective in driving a wedge between labor and environmental groups (Kazis and Grossman 1991).

Tensions grew especially intense after the first round of oil price spikes that occurred in the early 1970s. During this period, corporations began to explicitly tie job losses to environmental regulations. The Ford Motor Company, for instance, released a study claiming that 75,000 auto jobs would be lost if the 1977 Clean Water Act amendments were approved. These corporate arguments were further elaborated in conservative think tanks, and echoed by the media. By the late 1970s, many unions had become convinced that there was a severe environment/jobs trade-off, and they reversed many of their positions on environmental protection.

However, within a decade it had become clear that unions had not managed to protect themselves by adopting anti-environmental positions. The 1980s demonstrated that massive job losses, wage stagnation, and union busting are fully consistent with accelerated ecological destruction. As a result, by the 1990s union leaders and the rank and file had begun to return to a more activist stance against corporate power. The painful lessons of the 1980s made the emergence of a green-blue coalition in the 1990s possible. Moreover, when critical analysis of trade liberalization regimes revealed the dual threat of massive job loss and greatly accelerated environmental destruction, the stage was set for a convergence of green and blue interests in Seattle.

Just as the American labor movement went through important transformations in the post WWII era, so too did the mainstream environmental movement. During the late 1960s and early 1970s, an ecology movement emerged that was rooted in the new suburban middle class (Hurley 1995). The mainstream U.S. ecology movement brought issues such as municipal waste, population, pollution, and extinction to the U.S. political agenda. However, it failed to address the unequal distribution of ecological costs and benefits by race and class.

It fell to other groups, which came to be called environmental justice organizations, to broaden ecological agendas to incorporate race and class issues. Emerging out of the civil rights movement, environmental justice organizations came to demand equal environmental protection for communities of color. This environmental justice movement has therefore challenged mainstream environmental activists to integrate social justice concerns into the environmental agenda.[5]

The environmental justice movement emerged simultaneously, and in dialogue with, an anti-toxics movement that was rooted in white, working class communities. The anti-toxics movement developed out of local contamination episodes such as that at Love Canal. Like the early labor and more recent environmental justice movements, the anti-toxics movement focuses on public health concerns. These locally organized environmental groups have sometimes employed the civil disobedience tactics used by civil rights organizations and organized labor in earlier struggles, drawing on a tradition of working class political activism.[6]

In short, there are a number of different types of labor and environmental activism in the United States. And the possibilities for generating linkages between workers and environmentalists are different, depending on what specific groups are involved. It is therefore necessary to examine, in a bit more detail, where the real possibilities exist to tie segments of the union and environmental movements together in enduring coalitions.

---

[5] Bullard (1990); Bryant and Mohai (1992); Cole and Foster (2000).
[6] Levine (1982); Brown and Mikkelson (1990); Szasz (1994).

Problems and Promise in the Blue/Green Coalition

Under what conditions do social movement organizations form stable coalitions? While little empirical work has addressed this question, the academic literature suggests that a number of conditions must come together to make alliances work.

Whether or not coalitions form depends to a significant extent on the external political environment. Analyses of peace, pro-life, and labor-community movements, for example, suggest that coalitions are more likely to form when there is a specific political threat or a new opportunity.[7] Indeed, many of the recent efforts to create labor-environment alliances were prompted by external events. The convening of the WTO summit in Seattle, for instance, provided a unique opportunity for workers and environmentalists to join in temporary actions.

Meanwhile, there are significant obstacles to coalition formation (Hathaway and Meyer 1993/4). One problem has to do with organizational resources. It is difficult for an organization to enter into broader coalitions if it is losing money and members. This partly explains why unions retreated from environmental issues in the 1980s, as they entered into a precipitous decline (Moberg 1999). The organizational needs of unions during that time made coalition building extremely difficult.

Some of the leaders in labor-environmental organizations are aware of this problem. For example, an online guide from Friends of the Earth notes: "Building a coalition can increase the impact of an individual organization's efforts. There are also disadvantages. Being a member of a coalition can divert time and resources from your other work" (Friends of the Earth).

Another challenge to coalition building is that potentially allied organizations must have at least partially overlapping ideologies. This poses difficulties for building links between mainstream labor and environmental organization, which often have very different views about the value of economic growth, industrial development, and natural resource extraction. On the other hand, it may be easier to build alliances between unions and environmental justice groups, given their similar concerns about pollution exposure. Of course, uneasy discussions may have to occur over the issue of race if these alliances are to endure.

---

[7] Estabrook et al. (2000); Hathaway and Meyer (1993/4); Staggenborg (1986).

Another piece of the puzzle involves the work that must be done between organizations. Fred Rose's (2000) work on coalitions among the peace, labor, and environmental movements has pointed out the key role that "bridge builders" play. These are "people who are comfortable and competent to act within diverse social classes" (Rose 2000: 167). Rose argues that the labor and environmental movements have different class bases, and different organizational cultures. Labor organizations tend to operate with hierarchical models, whereas environmentalists usually employ consensus models for defining tactics and goals. As a result, individuals in these groups have difficulty communicating. Bridge-builders can sometimes ease the communications between these distinct groups, although these differences generally remain a source of tension.

In some circumstance, factors like timing, organizational resources, overlapping ideologies and successful communication come together to foster the creation of coalitions. But, once in existence, these coalitions are still subject to additional pressures that either help sustain, or help destroy, coalitions. Staggenborg (1986) argues, for instance, that coalitions are more likely to endure if external funding can be secured to support alliance-maintenance work. This observation seems to be borne out in the labor/environment coalition. For instance, the Just Transition Alliance succeeded in winning foundation support for its work in building links between labor, environmental, and community groups. This has helped the alliance engage in the longer-term work that is needed to solidify connections between organizations that often have different cultures, styles, and objectives.

In our opinion, the challenge of fashioning a blue-green coalition in the United States must be framed in terms of what streams of American environmentalism are most compatible with the agenda of organized labor. Perhaps the most viable long-term coalitions can be formed between labor and the environmental justice/anti-toxics streams of U.S. environmentalism.[8] At least historically, these groups share similar structural positions in the political economy and similar analyses of power, which has led them to make similar tactical choices. It is also worth remembering that the Reverend Dr. Martin Luther King Jr. was assassinated while supporting striking sanitation workers, which meant that he himself was fusing civil rights, labor and environmental concerns at the end of his life.

---

[8] Gould, Schnaiberg and Weinberg (1996); Pellow and Park (2002).

Another aspect of coalition building involves ensuring that each member of the alliance is helping the other. In the blue/green coalition, there seem to be important imbalances in this regard. Labor participation in environmental causes has been fairly common, especially at the local level. But environmentalists have not generally protested plant closings, wage stagnation, or other things that are important to workers. In short, environmentalists have been silent on key labor concerns, while they have expected unflinching support from labor for their own agenda.

It could be argued, in fact, that US environmentalists have been poor coalition partners. To improve their appeal to labor, environmental groups will have to articulate policies that allow for sustainable industrial growth, job expansion, and just transitions to renewable energy, among other things. So, part of the challenge of forging an enduring blue/green coalition in the United States involves convincing environmentalists that they have to extend more assistance to working people.

There are a series of instances in which local environmental groups have begun working with unionized labor to achieve common objectives. For instance, when a Louisiana BASF facility locked out its workers in the mid-1980s, the union started looking for local allies. The union established contacts with local environmental justice groups, who had long been active in the infamous "cancer alley" between Baton Rouge and New Orleans. This join effort against the company has forged lasting relations between workers and environmentalists at the local level.[9]

Although some analysts argue that it will be easier to create alliances on the local level, there are also reasons to expect that national-level connections can also be forged. Brian Obach (1999, 2000) argues that coalitions can be created in Washington DC, since union and environmental staff members are living very similar lives. He argues that these movement staffers often have broader knowledge of issues than any local membership, and may be able to think beyond the rough "transition" times that arise in campaigns.

If it is still unclear whether coalitions can be more easily forged at the local or national levels, the challenges become even more complex when efforts are undertaken to create alliances at the global level. It is important to note that there are many cases in which transnational networks have succeeded in exerting real power – especially on policies undertaken by governments

---

[9] Roberts and Toflolon-Weiss (2001); Minchin (2003).

in developing countries. For instance, the creation of extractive reserves in Brazil – where sustainable harvesting is conducted while ecosystems are protected – was prompted in part by the efforts of international environmental campaigns (Keck and Sikkink 1998). In this case, the Brazilian government was forced to accede to combined demands from Brazilian activists, and a strong international movement of support.

While there are cases in which international alliances have succeeded in working well, it is still a difficult arena in which to operate. If cultural and class divisions cause problems in alliances at the level of the United States, these divisions can be even more problematic when people from different countries try to coordinate their activities. One axis of tension at the international level, for instance, has emerged between reformist and more radical or even revolutionary activists. As of yet, there is no real agreement on whether anti-globalization campaigns should have as their long-term goal the reformation or abolition of global institutions like the WTO, the World Bank, or the IMF. Analysts that lump all oppositional movements together into a single phenomenon risk overlooking these crucial internal debates, and missing the challenges involved in forging an enduring coalition at the global level.

Whither the Blue/Green Coalition?

In the aftermath of the 9/11 attacks, the American wing of the "anti-globalization" movement has at least temporarily shifted strategies so as to not appear unpatriotic. Domestic dissent has been more intensely repressed by an increasingly authoritarian state, while activists have also self-policed their demonstrations out of a fear of alienating mainstream society (LeClerc and Gould 2003). Unfortunately, the combination of state repression and self policing may have negative consequences for the fate of the blue-green coalition.

The effort to moderate the rhetoric and tactics of the anti-corporate globalization movement in the United States has marginalized the more "radical" elements of the environmental and labor movements. These groups, though, have offered the clearest structural critiques of neo-liberalism. And these more radical groups have most strongly championed the need to create and sustain a strong coalition between organized labor and environmentalists. Yet these voices are being at least partially silenced in the post 9/11 period. As a result, efforts to rebuild and sustain a blue-green coalition which challenges the current global development trajectory have been weakened to the point of near invisibility.

Will mainstream environmental groups be interested in reviving efforts to forge a long-term coalition with workers? Evidence suggests that the "Big 10" groups are deeply split over this issue. More conservative groups like the National Wildlife Federation, the World Wildlife Fund, and the Nature Conservancy appear to be uninterested in sustaining such a coalition. More radical groups, such as the Sierra Club and Friends of the Earth, have already said yes. For instance, the Sierra Club ran a major piece entitled "Green + Blue = Powerful Alliance" in its newsletter *The Planet* in June 2002. "Developing relationships with unions can be tricky," the article reads. "Who do you talk to? The best way to get access is through another labor leader. Face time matters. Don't just e-mail them or phone them" (Sierra Club 2002). At the bottom of the article is a notice stating that Sierra Club staff are represented by two unions.

Even within the Sierra Club, though, there are different stances about the blue/green coalition. Those who focus on preservation and anti-logging campaigns, for instance, are less supportive of a pro-worker swing. On the other hand, some within the organization have worked to increase the group's connections with environmental justice and toxics issues. Indeed, the Sierra Club committed itself to raise funds to pursue these kinds of campaigns at its 2000 annual meeting of the Board of Directors. They also held their 2001 annual meeting at the Mexican border, and examined labor/environmental issues at great length. Activists in these sections of the Sierra Club are more supportive of the blue/green coalition. Although no systematic surveys have been conducted, our belief is that the preservationist wing is stronger than the environmental justice camp within the Sierra Club. So, even within this organization, more work needs to be done before strong support emerges for a unified commitment to any blue/green coalition.

The divergent class origins of American labor organizing and environmentalism also continue to present major obstacles to the creation of a successful blue-green coalition. On the one hand, working people have always had some need to focus on protecting the health and well being of their local communities. Consequently, the labor movement has often addressed problems of pollution. On the other hand, a key focus of middle class and elite environmentalists has been on preserving wilderness areas, and on protecting the integrity of wilderness ecosystems. The relatively privileged class background of many mainstream environmentalists has allowed them to neglect working class pollution problems, and focus on non-human ecology concerns.

This suggests that a key problem in forging a blue/green coalition does not lie in increasing working class environmentalism – since this already exists to a certain extent. Instead, the focus may need to be on fostering more concern for working class people among relatively privileged environmentalists. Forging a lasting coalition between blues and mainstream greens will require that green organizations emphasize the environmental health of people more centrally in their projects.

Unfortunately, most mainstream environmental organizations remain committed to traditional preservation and conservation programs. It may be difficult for mainstream green leaders to move away from a focus on favored species and vistas, since that could alienate the upper class members that provide most of their funding. Shifting toward a stronger emphasis on environmental justice and public health concerns may erode the core constituency of mainstream environmental groups.

There are other structural difficulties that may hinder changes within mainstream environmental organizations. For instance, many directors of mainstream green organizations are themselves corporate executives (Dowie 1995). And a large amount of funding comes from corporate shareholders, who increase profits (and then donations) as they carry out the downsizing and relocation agendas that hurt American workers.

Mainstream green leaders may then be faced with a difficult choice. They can continue to rely primarily on financial support from corporate donors, which keeps them in a compromised position vis-à-vis labor. Or they can align their campaigns more closely with labor, and risk eroding their support in the corporate world. Mainstream environmental organizations are not likely to take the financially more risky option, unless they become convinced that key policy battles can only be won with the strong support of the labor movement.

As mentioned earlier, forging a blue-green alliance between workers and the environmental justice/anti-toxics movements presents fewer ideological obstacles. The people-centered environmentalism pursued by alternative greens, and the class similarities that exist between these activists and workers, will presumably ease conflicts.

It is possible that the concept of the "just transition" may provide a foundation on which to build the blue/green coalition over the medium to long term. According to the Public Health Institute, "a just transition calls for financing a fair and equitable transition for workers and communities in environmentally sensitive industries as we move towards more sustainable production."[10] The just transition concept argues that any transition to a sustainable economy should be carried out in such a way that costs are shared across society, and that the needs of workers are taken into consideration.

Leaders in the just transition movement have come mostly from labor. A key advocate of the approach has been the Oil, Chemical and Atomic Workers Union (which has joined with paper workers and is now called the PACE International Union). This group has made connections with the "public health" side of environmentalism, as well as with some environmental justice groups.

At the national level, the concept is promoted by the Just Transition Alliance. The JTA brings environmental justice groups and labor unions together for education, training and organizing workshops (Just Transition Alliance 2002). Other important groups include the Alliance for Sustainable Jobs and the Environment, and the Blue-Green Working Group. The successful formation of umbrella groups like these are considered to be one of the essential components to coalition success (Staggenborg 1986).

There are other promising developments at the national level. In February 2002, for instance, the Center for a Sustainable Economy and the Economic Policy Institute produced a report entitled "Clean Energy and Jobs: A Comprehensive Approach to Climate Change." This report offered evidence that a just transition toward a more efficient and sustainable energy system could be achieved while new jobs were created and dislocated workers were supported. In a hopeful sign of convergence, both the Sierra Club and the Service Employees International Union endorsed the report (Hoerner and Phelps 2002).

Clearly, there are some indications that a lasting blue/green coalition can be constructed in the United States, and perhaps on a broader level. Difficult

---

[10] For more information consult: http://www.justtransition.org.

challenges remain at the local, national, and international levels, of course. Still, we see many promising projects emerging, including the JTA, the Climate Justice movement, the Global Exchange organization, and the Corporate Watch group. Although the Turtle/Teamsters alliance that emerged on the streets in Seattle proved to be susceptible to strains, these continuing efforts to strengthen the coalition are certainly encouraging.

Frederick Buttel and Kenneth Gould

Global Social Movements at the Crossroads: An Investigation of Relations Between the Anti-Corporate Globalization and Environmental Movements[1]

Introduction

One of the most distinctive aspects of late-twentieth century globalization is that many of its predominant features are being challenged by a global-scale social movement, the anti-corporate globalization movement. Previous periods of globalization involved only modest social movements aimed at curbing one or another of the processes of international integration – with the partial exception of attempts to create an international working class or socialist movement. Today, though, a growing number of social scientists and activists believe that social movements must necessarily be global in their vision and scope if they are to be successful at challenging global capitalism (O'Brien et al. 2000).

The transnational reach of corporations and institutions such as the World Trade Organization, the World Bank, and the International Monetary Fund implies that effective challenges must likewise be

[1] This research was supported by the Center for World Affairs and the Global Economy, University of Wisconsin, Madison. Jonathan London and Patrick Jobes provided helpful comments on an earlier version of this chapter. The authors also wish to acknowledge the incisive comments offered by Andrew D. Van Alstyne and anonymous reviewers on an earlier draft of this chapter, which helped us produce a stronger argument and deeper analysis.

organized at the global level. And, in recent years, such a global movement has been growing in influence. In fact, many argue that the anti-corporate globalization movement has become the most significant leftist movement of the new millennium, and that it has the potential to alter the course of social change in the decades that follow (Brecher et al. 2000). In this chapter, we review the history, current characteristics, and future prospects facing this multi-faceted movement for social justice on a global level.

Bases of the Anti-Corporate Globalization Movement

The anti-corporate globalization movement has not been formed de novo, but has instead drawn many of its adherents from groups and networks associated with previous social movements. The anti-corporate globalization movement is a coalition that includes activists from long-established human rights, labor, and anti-hunger organizations; and it also draws support from newer anti-sweatshop, debt relief, fair trade, and HIV/AIDS prevention organizations. The coalition also draws participants from a diversity of ideologies, including anarchists, socialists, liberal reformers, environmentalists, and others. What gives this "movement of movements" cohesion is a common critique of neo-liberal economic policies, the anti-democratic nature of international financial institutions, and the increasing power of transnational corporations.

The anti-corporate globalization movement has developed a somewhat unique organizational structure designed to facilitate the maintenance of this diverse coalition across ideological and geographic space. Most importantly, the coalition has a strong commitment to non-hierarchical and consensus based decision making strategies. When needed, delegates from diverse organizations join together to form councils where strategic and tactical decisions can be made. However, these councils operate without formal leaders or a clear organizational hierarchy, and they are typically open to participation by anyone. The use of electronic bulletin boards, email, and websites facilitates this work. This organizational structure ensures that all groups are able to participate in decision making, and thus prevents severe schisms from developing.

There are a number of factors that have led to the rise of this anti-corporate globalization movement. First, many citizens have reservations about subjecting their countries and themselves to the vagaries of distant, unelected, and unaccountable trade regimes. Increased dependence on trade can create social benefits, but it can also increase the movement of jobs offshore, rising unemployment, and the loss of worker protections. These trade-related potential threats have stimulated active resistance by many kinds of citizens throughout the world in recent decades.

Second, it often appears that institutions like the World Trade Organization and the North American Free Trade Agreement have allowed foreign legislators to veto domestic environmental, labor, or social welfare protections. Anti-corporate globalization activists frequently argue that trade regulations are creating a powerful "race to the bottom," as nation-states water down their domestic regulations in order to remain attractive for capital investment. The impacts of trade liberalization on domestic safety nets, and the discourses developed by the anti-corporate movement, have spurred greater mobilizations of citizens in many areas of the world.

There is also a significant degree of revulsion against the "McDonaldization" or Americanization of world culture which is thought to be associated with globalization (Ritzer 1993). The rise of the anti-corporate globalization movement is also partly fueled by a reaction against the perceived attempt by the United States to dominate global affairs in the wake of the collapse of the Soviet Union, and the relative absence of a countervailing world power. So, the movement has strong anti-US, and anti-imperialist dimensions to it as well.

While there is debate over the historical roots of the coalition, there is a surprising consensus about the growing influence of the anti-corporate globalization movement.[2] Global social movements appear in some cases to be better positioned than nationally based movements to advocate for environmental, labor, and social insurance protections. Indeed, movement proponents and a number of social-scientific analysts argue that global social movements have been very adept at creating coalitions that cross national borders. At the same time, movement opponents are fearful that these kinds

---

[2] There is debate over the most suitable terminology for describing this movement. The movement's opponents are most likely to refer to the movement as the "anti-trade movement" suggesting, somewhat inaccurately, that anti-corporate globalization movement supporters object to international trade or globalization as a whole. Many movement supporters strongly reject the "anti-globalization" label. They often conceptualize their movement as a manifestation of "globalization from below," in contrast to a transnational, elite-dominated, "top-down" globalization regime. There is also considerable disagreement as to whether the most suitable terminology is that which pronounces the movement's radical sentiments, or that which sounds more moderate.

of successes will create a tidal wave of "mindless" opposition to the fragile institutions that now facilitate freer trade.[3]

Analysts believe these movements can be influential because dominant actors are vulnerable to the scrutiny and hostility that can be generated within societies and governments by negative public opinion.[4] Global social movements can also be influential because they combine the organizational strengths of long-established environmental and development-justice NGOs, and the strong allegiances that are often found in new social movements or identity-driven groups.[5]

There are other key properties of the anti-corporate globalization movement that must also be highlighted. We should recognize that the lion's share of protests have occurred in the global South, for instance.[6] Protests have been particularly common in Bolivia, Argentina, Thailand, Ecuador, India, Brazil, and Indonesia. And, on May 1, 2000, there were anti-corporate globalization protests in about 75 cities on six continents across the world. Moreover, southern activists are generally more radical and confrontational than their counterparts in the North.

While acknowledging this point, though, our guess is that anti-corporate globalization protests in the North are in some respects the more influential segment of the movement. This is because northern activists have the socio-economic and geographical capacity to more directly attack transnational institutions – and to gain the attention of the heads of state of the countries that have dominant voices within these institutions. In a general sense, activist dynamics in both the global north and south appear to be mutually-reinforcing and important to the success of the coalition.

Another source of power is the extent to which many different kinds of groups work together to get organizational and outreach work accomplished. The anti-corporate globalization movement, for example, is now endorsed in

---

[3] In addition to the pronouncements of Thomas Friedman, perhaps the most poignant example of this is the speech of C. Fred Bersgten, a tireless supporter of trade liberalization, entitled "The Backlash Against Globalization," at the April 2000 Meeting of the Trilateral Commission in Tokyo, in which he said candidly that "anti-globalization forces are now in ascendancy."

[4] O'Brien et al. (2001); Cohen and Rai (2000).

[5] Taylor (1995); Brulle (2000); Schnaiberg and Gould (2000).

[6] Protests against the Bretton Woods institutions, and IMF structural adjustment policies in particular, have been a fairly regular feature of political conflict in the global South for well over 25 years (Walton and Seddon, 1994). See Podobnik (2001) and Smith (2002) for analyses of the more recent dimensions of these protests.

the publications and on the home pages of a vast array of NGOs and related movements. A wide variety of environmental, agricultural, labor, consumer, human rights, women's rights, animal rights, and related groups now also have "trade" or "globalization analyst" staffers. So, anti-corporate globalization events and campaigns can be undertaken using the expertise, energy, and resources that exist in this wide array of affiliated organizations.

Much of the ideological coherence of the movement is also provided by a small group of prominent intellectual figures (e.g., Walden Bello, José Bové, Vandana Shiva, Robert Weissman, Naomi Klein, Kevin Danaher, and Lori Wallach), all of whom are associated with these distinct NGOs. Moreover, these NGOs turn out a large number of their members at anti-corporate globalization protests, and probably many-fold more sympathizers who visit their websites.[7]

Once planning for a protest is underway, the movement can draw on this diverse organizational and intellectual milieu. Protest organizing mostly occurs by way of internet websites, email, and chat rooms, which eliminates the need for centralized control and reduces resource costs. Instead, specific organizations are temporarily created to coordinate planning for particular protests. Months prior to a protest independent clusters and affinity groups form to organize traveling road shows and teach-ins throughout the host country. The internet is used intensively at this stage.

Once a protest is underway, cell phones become the principal means of communication. Indeed, protesters with cell phones are sometimes able to outmaneuver law enforcement and security personnel. The internet and cell phone modalities of protest organization have facilitated the accommodation of considerable diversity within the movement. The lack of direct contact among these various groups tends to militate against infighting, but also requires an acceptance of a certain degree of ideological and tactical plurality. Stressing the diversity that has been accommodated within the street protest component of the movement, Väryrnen (2000) goes so far as to refer to anti-corporate globalization movements in the plural.[8]

---

[7] Press accounts and participant observation indicate that the following groups are relatively consistently represented at anti-corporate globalization protests in the advanced countries: developed-country trade unions such as the AFL-CIO, Rainforest Action Network, Sierra Club, Global Exchange, Alliance for Global Justice, Direct Action Network, Jubilee 2000, 50 Years is Enough, Radical Roots, Ruckus Society, People for the Ethical Treatment of Animals (PETA), and Co-Motion Action.

[8] Crossley (2002) concurs, and goes so far as to say that anti-corporate globaliza-

Another characteristic of the movement appears to be a tendency for many of its most active participants, particularly in protest actions, to be young. In general, the majority of movement participants tend to have a social structural profile similar to that of the "new class," the presumed base of support of so-called new social movements (Scott 1990). However, protest organizers and leaders in some organizations tend to be substantially older, as are the participants representing organized labor.

Finally, the anti-corporate globalization movement finds itself being defined both advantageously and destructively by the mainstream press. The size and scope of protest events have been significantly shaped by press attention. Pre-protest publicity in the press tends to increase the size of protests; more press attention attracts more supporters and onlookers, which attracts more press attention, and so on. Interestingly, the 1999 Seattle protest received some positive mainstream press commentary for having raised issues of concern to many U.S. and world citizens. More recently, though, the mainstream press' treatment of the anti-corporate globalization movement has tended to cast the movement in an unfavorable light. What is most often emphasized now are violent protesters, anarchist groups using "Black Bloc" tactics, and youthful participants who would rather demonstrate than negotiate. The media often now portrays the movement's message as incoherent and indecipherable, rather than as providing a multi-faceted critique of neoliberal forms of globalization.

One of the basic arguments of this chapter is that there has been coalescence of a good many global social movements under the banner of the anti-corporate globalization movement. But we feel that an assessment of the current status and future role of this coalition hinges on the articulations that occur between the global environmental movement and the anti-corporate globalization movement. The role that environmental claims and strategies play in the anti-corporate globalization movement's "repertoire of contention" will be critical to the movement's future (Tilly 1986).

tion activism and protest are a "protest field" rather than a movement per se, on account of their highly fluid character. We largely agree with Crossley's characterization of global anti-corporate struggle.

Antecedents of the Anti-Corporate Globalization Movement

While there is yet only a modest literature on the anti-corporate globalization movement, the literature that exists[9] has suggested a variety of historical tributaries to the movement. Some of the key historical antecedents include the late 1960s New Left and the Paris protests of 1968, the NGO activism leading up to the 1992 Earth Summit in Rio de Janeiro, and the Zapatista uprising in Chiapas, Mexico, during the mid-1990s. While not denying that these antecedents may have played some role, we maintain that there were four particularly critical developments that led up to the debut of the mass anti-corporate globalization movement in Seattle in 1999. Let us review these events.

In the 1990s, a series of WTO trade rulings appeared to prioritize trade liberalization over the environmental and health concerns of citizens in the global north. One trade ruling determined that U.S. restrictions on Mexican tuna imports were unlawful, even though the restriction was meant to ensure that only dolphin-safe tuna was brought into the U.S. Another ruling then overturned a U.S. ban on shrimp imports from countries whose nets kill sea turtles. The WTO also ruled that an American ban on highly-polluting gasoline was impermissible, while a NAFTA lawsuit was brought against the state of California for its ban on the polluting gasoline additive MTBE. As the end of the 1990s approached, it was also becoming clear that the environmental side-agreements to NAFTA were ineffective.

The importance of these anti-environmental rulings cannot be overstated. Until these rulings, many mainstream US environmental groups had remained largely neutral in trade debates. But these new rulings shook environmental groups to their foundations. It became apparent that a domestic environmental regulation may not be very effective unless its scope can be extended to cover the conditions of production of imported goods. Further, it seemed that the WTO was giving foreign governments and corporations the power to overturn domestic environmental legislation under some circumstances. As a result, there was a significant shift in the center of gravity of mainstream environmental NGO opinion about globalization in general, and trade liberalization in particular. By early 1999, moderate environmental groups had

---

[9] Cf. Brecher (2000); Danaher and Burbach (2000); Danaher (2001); Dunkley (2000); O'Brien et al. (2001); Starr (2000); Epstein (2001); George et al. (2001).

joined Friends of the Earth, the Sierra Club, Greenpeace, and Public Citizen in taking a critical stance toward corporate globalization.

There was a simultaneous set of revelations about labor conditions in export processing zones that also shook the confidence of consumers in affluent countries. In 1996, for instance, Kathie Lee Gifford was forced to admit that clothing sold with her name was manufactured in foreign factories that had very bad work and safety conditions. Similar revelations about work conditions in factories that supplied Nike, Reebok, and other sporting goods manufactureres gave added momentum to an emergent anti-sweatshop movement (see Ross, this volume). This new movement dramatized the social impacts that corporations could generate as they shifted production facilities to low-wage countries in the global south.

At the same time, the Asian financial crisis of 1997 created something of a crisis of legitimacy for the trade liberalization agenda (Stiglitz 2003). The crisis demonstrated to many state officials, analysts, and activists in the South that the "big three" globalization institutions – the IMF, the World Bank, and WTO – had less regard for the well-being of people in developing countries than for international monetary stability.

Finally, the explosion of public opposition to genetically modified (GM) foods in Europe created problems for the WTO. WTO rules suggested that the EU would have little legal basis for excluding GMO agricultural input products and GM foods. But European public resistance to these technologies was so strong that the EU had little choice but to oppose the WTO rules. This GMO controversy galvanized the anti-WTO sentiments of many farm and consumer groups across Western Europe, East Asia, and other areas.

All of these events combined to help forge a multi-faceted coalition that focused on the 1999 WTO ministerial meeting in Seattle. The coalition included anti-corporate globalization groups, environmental organizations, organized labor, anti-GMO groups, development activist/world hunger groups, animal rights groups, religious organizations, and activists and officials from many countries of the South. Perhaps the most telling symbol of the Seattle coalition was the poster which read, "Teamsters and Turtles – Together At Last." Indeed, what made the Seattle WTO protest so path breaking was the apparent environmentalization of the anti-corporate globalization movement. The strong environmental overtone of the Seattle protest was among the major factors that conferred on it a certain legitimacy among the U.S. public – and among the citizenries elsewhere among the OCED countries – and that contributed to some favorable press coverage of the protest.

Numerous anti-corporate globalization rallies and protests across the world occurred after 1999 as well. During the period 1999–2001, cities such as Washington, Prague, Quebec, Genoa, Melbourne, and Gothenburg witnessed repeated clashes between coalitions of protesters and the security personnel who were deployed to protect state officials and corporate leaders (see Podobnik, this volume). However, since the terrorist attacks on the World Trade Center and Pentagon on September 11, 2001, protests in some regions have been more muted.

A conscious decision was made on the part of many U.S. anti-corporate globalization activists, for instance, to take a less aggressive tack in order to distance themselves from the terrorist attacks. The U.S. part of the movement has also decreased protest activity because of an increase in state repression – which has been facilitated by mechanisms such as the USA PATRIOT Act. The Justice Department's new capacity to monitor social movement organizations has caused most anti-corporate globalization activists to increase their own internal security measures, decrease the volume of accessible communications, and self-censor their expression of ideas on movement actions and tactics. The detention of anti-corporate globalization activists at the U.S.-Canadian border, and the denial of flying rights to some activists, further disrupted movement organizing.

Another factor was the major shift in the U.S. political climate following September 11, 2001. A surge of nationalism that was openly hostile to dissent of any type led to a certain protest paralysis, and the number of movement sympathizers willing to overtly express political dissent rapidly decreased. As of this writing, the U.S. wing of the movement has yet to return to the more aggressive tone that typified protests from late 1999 through late 2001.[10]

Dilemmas Facing the Anti-Corporate Globalization Movement

The anti-corporate globalization movement is currently the most important global-scale movement of the left. The movement has registered some major successes in recent years. As is expanded upon below, it has led to concessionary responses from various quarters of the "big three," particularly the World Bank. Moreover, it has forced international financial institutions to

---

[10] Although mass peaceful protest has returned on less complex issues, most notably the war in Iraq and the Bush re-election campaign.

offer more rhetorical attention to issues of poverty alleviation, ecological sustainability, and the potentially negative results of some structural adjustment programs (such as those pursued in Argentina). The anti-corporate globalization movement has also been influential in helping to stiffen the EU's resolve to hold its ground on agricultural protections during Millennial Round negotiations (Burmeister et al., 2001). And the movement has complicated negotiations over the Free Trade for the Americas Act. But despite the movement's successes, it faces some very significant dilemmas.

Many of the dilemmas faced by the anti-corporate globalization movement reflect the kinds of debates that all mass movements have to confront. For instance, should the movement seek to transform or disable the main institutions of globalization? On one hand, the dominant institutions are deeply entrenched – and so some activists argue that it makes sense to try to reform them through conventional influence-mobilization approaches. Some reform-minded activists also hold out hope that the United Nations offers an institutional alternative to the IFIs, through which transnational economic relations may be mediated (Bello 2001). On the other hand, radical critics claim that dominant institutions are so invested in the neoliberal agenda that they will never respond meaningfully to the demands of a diverse array of NGOs and civil society groups. This is one key debate that is yet to be resolved within the anti-corporate globalization movement.

The anti-corporate globalization movement also has to face hard questions about where its component groups get monetary and organizational resources to undertake long-term movement building. Protest mobilizations undertaken to this point appear to have required relatively few resources, and they have not had to turn to major foundations or other institutions for funding. On the other hand, the vast network of NGOs that have given support to particular mobilizations do get their own money from individual donations and foundation grants. The Pew, MacArthur, and Ford foundations, among many others, have provided resources to NGOs such as Friends of the Earth, Global Exchange, and Oxfam which have allowed these groups to weigh in on trade, globalization, and environmental policy debates. Although modest, this foundation support has already attracted the attention of the right-wing Capital Research Center – which is now trying to stop these contributions.

The Capital Research Center may not itself change foundation priorities; nevertheless, it is clear that foundations can be fickle in their funding priorities, and so this modest source of support is unreliable. The de-funding of this component of the movement will probably not deter protests, but it is likely to reduce mainstream NGO participation over time. This reduced engagement by mainstream groups will presumably permit the anti-corporate globalization movement to generate a more clearly articulated anti-capitalist ideology, which appeals to some activists. On the other hand, such an ideological turn may significantly reduce its appeal to many citizens across the global north. An ideological radicalization of the movement could also lead to political marginalization, which would increase the capacity of neoliberals and their media allies to discredit the movement altogether (Ackerman, 2001). In summary, the uncertainty of funding sources – and related debates over the reformist/radical nature of the movement – are yet to be fully addressed by movement participants.

While some of these dilemmas are faced by all large-scale social movements, the anti-corporate globalization movement also faces challenges that are specific to itself. One unique dilemma concerns violence and so-called Black Bloc tactics.[11] Violence does attract public and media attention, which some claim is a good thing. However, press coverage of violent events is almost always negative – regardless of whether the violence is initiated by the police or the protesters. Indeed, evidence suggests that mainstream citizens in the United States are less supportive of protests that become violent in the post 9/11 period than they were in the past. As a result, many mainstream movement participants are trying to distance themselves from violent tactics and their proponents in the anarchist community. They instead generally suggest that future protests should stress community based actions at the local level. Others argue that a diversity of tactics, defined and carried out by semi-independent groups, should be used. Regardless, debates over the role of violence and property destruction are yet to be resolved.

Another significant dilemma concerns the long-term nature of the movement's coalition and ideology. The movement has undergone a shift in its composition and discourse since 1999. While environmental groups played a central role in the Seattle protests, more recently there has been a decline in the movement's focus on environmental issues. Instead, there has been a shift toward social justice and global inequality themes. The Genoa G8 protest

---

[11] The "Black Bloc" is the most frequently referenced anarchist group involved in anti-corporate globalization protests, though there are numerous other anarchist groups as well (Epstein 2001). See also Starr (this volume).

in 2001, for instance, exhibited a new emphasis on global-scale dimensions of inequality.[12]

It can be argued that there are good reasons for bringing issues of global inequality to our collective attention, even if that implies a reduction in focus on environmental topics. Williams (2001) has suggested that WTO officials now appear to be bending over backwards to avoid making new anti-environmental rulings that threaten regulations in the global north. So, environmental threats may be temporarily reduced in North American and Western Europe. At the same time, though, there is growing evidence that IMF-imposed structural adjustment policies (SAPs) are wreaking social and environmental damage throughout the global south. An increased focus on the human and ecological impacts of SAPs in the developing world is therefore needed. Moreover, this new focus may help sustain north-south connections within the coalition.

This shift to a focus on social and environmental destruction in the global south is also consistent with a shift away from a concentration on the WTO, and toward a renewed targeting of the IMF and the World Bank. The environmental records of these two institutions are actually more troubling than that of the WTO. The social impacts of IMF austerity programs can be quite dramatic. Even the neo-liberal proponent Jeffrey Sachs has expressed the view that the IMF essentially functions as the debt collection enforcer of private banks, and that the IMF has sacrificed the economic recovery of many countries in the South. Meanwhile, the ecological damage wrought by World Bank projects is etched in the lands of many countries. In contrast to the often complicated and obscure impacts of WTO rulings, IMF/World Bank interventions can be documented in quite dramatic ways. And the IMF and World Bank are also more accessible to northern movement activists than the WTO, since they have offices in Washington, DC. As a result, this shift in targets makes sense on a variety of strategic levels.

The de-environmentalization of movement discourses, and the rise of issues relating to social justice and global inequality, raises a major dilemma however. The current core of the movement – which primarily consists of a com-

---

[12] This may represent a divergence in emphasis between North American and European wings of the anti-corporate globalization movement, or may represent a broader shift in transnational movement ideology. A European book produced by the anti-corporate globalization movement, subtitled "A Guide to the Movement", fails to list environmentalists or environmental organizations in the section addressing the key "Actors" in the coalition (George et al. 2001).

mitted group of young radicals who are concerned about inequality and ecological destruction across the world – is not large enough to effect real policy changes. While these kinds of activists are attracted by campaigns that
focus on social and ecological turmoil in the global south, these themes are
not likely to appeal to broad constituencies in countries of the north. Instead,
Seattle-era discourses that emphasized the ways in which WTO rulings threaten
domestic jobs and health in the north may need to be retained as key themes
if the anti-corporate globalization movement is to attract large numbers of
new adherents in affluent countries.

It seems apparent that the anti-corporate globalization movement will need
to be a coalitional movement that simultaneously prioritizes labor, environmental, and social justice issues if it is to have a chance of achieving its goals.[13]
This kind of broad coalition, in constant internal dialogue, is needed in order
to generate a coherent yet inclusive movement ideology and rhetoric. Such
a coalition requires a focus on neoliberal policy impacts on domestic regulations, in addition to a focus on north-south equity issues. We believe that a
focus on neoliberalism can provide the ideological glue that can be capable
of fusing the concerns of diverse coalition participants into a common movement. The connections between transnational processes and domestic events
must be made clear to citizens across the world – and especially within the
G8 countries that exert most influence over international financial institutions.

While we believe it is possible to generate a broad ideological approach
that unifies many groups, we also want to highlight some of the policy dilemmas that remain to be addressed. For instance, the desire of many northern
activists to add labor and environmental standards to the WTO has already
raised concerns in the global south.

Remember, again, that the WTO rulings that overrode U.S. environmental
laws were the result of complaints filed by developing country governments
(Williams 2001). It remains to be seen how these policy dilemmas can be
negotiated within the anti-corporate globalization movement.

In a strategic sense, the political success of the movement will depend on
whether it can help induce two blocs of nation-states to resist a deepening
of the WTO agenda. Some countries of the global south may be encouraged
by anti-corporate globalization protests to demand major revisions in WTO
rules during its Millennial Round. In the previous round of WTO negotiations,

---

[13] Epstein (2001), Gould, Lewis and Roberts (2004).

developing countries signed away their rights to use protective trade policies as a means of industrialization. Governments of the south also agreed to open up their agricultural sectors to imports from agribusiness superpowers, while receiving few benefits of liberalized markets in the north.[14] And, continuing debt payment transfers from south to north are generating turmoil within many countries. For these and other reasons, there is at least the possibility that some governments from the global south can be encouraged to resist further liberalization in their regions. For instance, the more overtly anti-neoliberal governments currently in office in Ecuador, Venezuela, Brazil, and elsewhere may occasionally lend their ideological support to the anti-corporate globalization movement's objectives. On the other hand, impoverished nations cannot easily afford to alienate the most powerful countries in the world-system – or agree to abide by a host of new labor and environmental standards. Given these contradictory pressures, it is possible – though not inevitable – that a bloc of developing countries may lend their voice to calls by anti-corporate globalization activists for significant reforms in the global trading system.

The other bloc of nation-states with a potential interest in significant WTO reform is that of the EU. Public support for the anti-corporate globalization movement's agenda – and for related agendas such as curbing GMOs – appears to be significantly stronger in the EU than in the U.S. WTO rebukes of a number of European environmental, trade, and social policies appear to have created a growing public view that the EU must stand up for the preservation of social, labor, and environmental protections. Recent U.S. unilateralism with regard to the Kyoto Protocol and the war against Iraq has further hardened anti-U.S. sentiment throughout Europe, which may carry over into WTO negotiations.

The anti-corporate globalization movement has not, to our knowledge, specifically endorsed EU proposals for including social and environmental considerations in upcoming WTO negotiations. And the fact that strong EU advocacy of including new considerations could derail the Millennial Round is no doubt music to the ears of the anti-corporate globalization movement. But, even if the trade round goes forward, it may be that the anti-corporate globalization movement can find some support for reforms in the position of the EU.

---

[14] Araghi (2002); Madley (2000).

Conclusion

The anti-corporate globalization movement has already achieved significant successes. International institutions now must meet in remote locations or behind immense fortifications. The movement has turned the lack of transparency of these institutions into an important public relations problem. And several of these institutions have been prompted to make changes in their discourses and practices to respond to criticisms raised in protests. Moreover, efforts to move forward on the Millennial Round of the WTO have been complicated by social pressures generated by the anti-corporate globalization movement.

Despite major gains, though, the movement faces important dilemmas about its ideological coherence, the tactics it endorses, and its long-term objectives. Given the coalitional nature of the movement, it will not make decisions in the same manner that most social movements do. The choices will not be made by some centralized leadership group, but will instead be made by many different groups who consider themselves to be part of the broader movement. It remains to be seen whether this consensus-based organizational model allows for resolution of key dilemmas, or encourages the fragmentation of the movement.

Some of the most difficult dilemmas facing this coalitional movement concern the discursive emphasis of the movement. Among the critical choices will be whether to emphasize labor and environmental protections for people in the North, or to focus on global inequalities and social justice problems that appeal to people in the South. This is not to suggest, of course, that it is impossible to articulate projects that appeal to both groups. The Fair Trade movement, for instance, strives to link concerned consumers in the North with peasants and artisans in the South (Dunkley 2000). But the fact that these kinds of north/south interactions are somewhat rare suggests that there is a strong element of truth to the notion that difficult choices will need to be made within the movement's highly decentralized structure.

As hard as it will be to cement alliances between northern and southern groups, it may be the best option available to the anti-corporate globalization movement. It is possible that mainstream environmental NGOs in the north will prove to be somewhat unreliable partners within the coalition. In the post-September 11th political climate, mainstream environmental organizations are more likely to resist confrontational tactics – and may instead seek accommodation with the transnational corporations and international financial organizations that the anti-corporate globalization movement aims to confront (Schnaiberg and Gould 2000).

If mainstream organizations prove to be unreliable partners, what other sources of support might there be? We suggest that stronger ties be forged between grassroots social and environmental justice groups that have pro-liferated in both the global north and south. By incorporating these new kinds of groups, an enduring movement focused on reducing inequalities in all regions of the world can perhaps be constructed. Attention to domestic inequal-ities could also help sustain a tenuous alliance with organized labor in the United States (see Gould et al. 2004). Such a focus could also draw stronger support from communities of color in the U.S., where minority participation in the anti-corporate globalization movement has been minimal (see Starr 2004).

A social and environmental justice frame might also allow the movement to define an agenda that sidesteps the environment vs. labor and social wel-fare trade-offs that often crop up in conventional debates. Finding an ideo-logical vision that links domestic socio-economic and environmental problems in the North, with similar problems in the south, will be crucial if the major components of the anti-corporate globalization movement are to be held together.

Of course, such a vision would not itself solve all the problems that would emerge if mainstream environmental groups withdrew from the anti-corpo-rate globalization coalition. Social and environmental justice groups in both the North and South are small, decentralized, and limited in financial terms. However, these groups tend to be more politically aggressive and active than mainstream organizations.[15] Their more radical analyses of power may also allow them to forge stronger links with anti-corporate members of the coalition.

For all its successes, the anti-corporate globalization movement faces real challenges in the coming years. How the coalition deals with possible shifts in allegiances of mainstream environmental groups is a key unknown. But even if mainstream groups distance themselves from the "movement of move-ments," there are alternative sources of support that can potentially be mobi-lized. What does seem clear, though, is that opportunities exist for the coalition to articulate ever-broader critiques of the negative social and environmental

---

[15] Bullard (1993); Taylor (1995); Gedicks (2001).

consequences of conventional forms of globalization. If new linkages can be forged between groups in the global north and south, it is possible that even greater pressure can be exerted across the world in the name of equality and sustainability.

Thomas Reifer

Torture, Human Rights and the Challenges Facing the Global Peace and Justice Movement

Introduction

As commentators have often noted, among the greatest challenges faced by popular opposition movements is the non-continuity of resistance. When one looks at some of the major movements of this century, we can see waves of popular protest, albeit with a changing emphasis. The global peace movement of the 1980s was followed by the uprisings in Eastern Europe leading to the collapse of the Soviet empire there and ultimately the breakup of the USSR, part of the larger wave of rebellion sweeping much of the semiperiphery and periphery during this period. Then, in the aftermath of the Soviet collapse, a new global justice movement targeting neoliberal globalization emerged.

To be sure, the new movement had important roots in previous history. Nevertheless, as the movement garnered steam, it had to deal with a fast changing international environment. Even before 9/11, the advent of the Bush administration signaled a change of emphasis among leading U.S. elites towards a more aggressive geopolitical strategy. 9/11 then provided a window of opportunity for the Bush Administration to carry out ambitious plans to secure the unrivalled dominance of U.S. state-corporate power networks in the global system. Many of these visions were laid out in the Project for the

New American Century, whose supporters were prominent in the Bush Administration.[1]

9/11, Iraq & the Current Conjuncture

The horrific terrorist attacks against the U.S. on September 11, 2001 greatly strengthened the hands of the most aggressive elements of U.S. elites. The attacks – a rude wakeup call for those who associated the era of neoliberal globalization with a new era of peaceful cooperation – were indicative of much broader trends. In recent decades we have seen what amounts of a global Islamist revival and insurgency, much of it non-violent, and directly against processes of neoliberal globalization and militarization, in the context of the increased U.S. military presence in the Persian Gulf. As many increasingly realize, such movements can take progressive forms or embrace reactionary strategies like the attacks on innocent non-combatants, as in 9/11.

Numerous scholars have analyzed the impact of neoliberal structural adjustment programs, U.S. military intervention and the U.S.-led organization of a global Isalmic jihad against the Soviet invasion of Afghanistan in the wake of the Iranian Revolution, in the resurgence of Islamist-based antisystemic movements in the modern world. Here, drawing on civilizational resources and religious beliefs, what we might call Islamist ethno-natioanlism has taken up the banner anti-imperialist mobilization heretofore carried out largely by secular nationalists.[2]

Instead of addressing the underlying structural bases of support for the revival of Islamist fundamentalism, the Bush administration's military adventures, most recently the invasion and occupation of Iraq, have provided Al Qaeda with a new generation of recruits (see NIC, 2004). Moreover, after 9/11, in a decision made January 18, 2002 and announced soon thereafter, the Bush administration took away the rights of protection offered by the Geneva Conventions – long considered the core of modern international humanitarian law – to members of Al Qaeda and the Taliban (a decision now extended to foreign fighters in Iraq), and recently indicated its desire to try and formally change Geneva to conform more towards U.S. current practices.[3]

---

[1] See http://www.newamericancentury.org/.
[2] See Lubeck and Reifer (2004); see also Burke (2004).
[3] See Gonzales (2002: 1); New York Times (1/8/05: A1); Los Angeles Times (1/7/05: A24).

The International Committee of the Red Cross, mandated with the task of monitoring compliance to the Geneva Conventions by the High Contracting Parties, immediately disagreed with the U.S. decision, arguing that both groups were protected under the Geneva Conventions, an opinion concurred in by other well respected legal scholars (Sloss, 2004).[4] Yet in practice these rights were effectively stripped from a much larger number of persons than just Al Qaeda and the Taliban.

The legal determinations of the Bush Administration were central in the widespread U.S. torture of detainees, in violation of the Geneva Conventions and the U.N. Convention Against Torture, and Other Cruel, Inhuman, or Degrading Treatment or Punishment, as first revealed to the global public at Abu Ghraib, Guantanamo, and numerous other locations. Since the U.S. is a signatory to both treaties, they are in the words of Article VI of the U.S. Constitution, "the Supreme Law of the Land" and therefore binding. In addition, as the Nuremberg trials showed, adherence to domestic law and orders is no defense against prosecution for War Crimes.[5]

In Abu Ghraib, torture, which is horrific in any event, was applied indiscriminately, even though according though U.S. military intelligence officers told the International Committee for the Red Cross that some 79 to 90% of those imprisoned had been mistakenly arrested after the U.S. invasion (Danner, 2004: 3). What the torture scandals, subsequent investigations and revelations have shown is how far the U.S. has moved from being a state that formally condemned torture "to one that practices torture routinely . . ."

---

[4] Others differ, arguing that though the Taliban is covered under Geneva as POWs, Al Qaeda, as a non-state group, is not; see in particular the piece by George H. Aldrich (2002). Aldrich was part of the Office of the General Counsel to the Secretary of Defense from 1960–65 and part of the Office of the Legal Adviser to the Secretary of State from 1965–77. Aldrich played a key role in the negotiations over Geneva Protocol I and II, which the U.S. signed, but which the Reagan Administration and those subsequent refused to ratify, with important members of the current Bush administration, such as Douglas Feith, speaking out against ratification (see Meron, 1998: ch. 8; see Aldrich, 2002: 896). Sloss (2004) presents a powerful argument for the applicability of the Geneva Conventions for both Al Qaeda and the Taliban. Jinks and Sloss (2004) present an equally compelling case that the U.S. President is legally bound by the conventions. For a review of the legality of the attack on Afghanistan in 2001 and the conflict there, see Mandel (2004).

[5] See the important piece by Scott Horton (2005), regarding the attempt by the commander of Auschwitz to argue that the abuses there were "excesses committed by individual prisoner guards," much like we have heard in regards to Abu Ghraib and other abuses. As Horton notes, U.S. prosecutors still held the German high command accountable for what were clearly outcomes of their earlier policy decisions, even in the absence of proof that the actual crimes took place with their knowledge. See also Jinks 2003, 2004.

(Danner, 2005: A 27).[6] To be sure, the U.S. has long supported and trained client states responsible for among the most egregious human rights abuses in the world, as in Central America. Yet with the move towards direct empire in Iraq, what is now being shown are U.S. citizen-soldiers and "corporate warriors" doing the work themselves, directly (see Singer, 2003, 2004a).

Since the torture scandal broke, formerly secret memorandums from high level members of the Bush administration have come to light which argue that the President has the executive authority as Commander in Chief to ignore treaties that the U.S. is a signatory of, from the Geneva Conventions to the U.N. Convention Against Torture, in the interests of protecting National Security. And in fact, administration officials took full advantage of the U.S. Senate's "'interrogator-friendly' definition of torture," to define the practice so narrowly so as to make clear examples of torture something else in legal terms; specifically, the U.S. Office of Legal Counsel of the Justice Department argued in a memo (only recently partially repudiated) that "acts must be of

---

[6] Danner (1/6/05, A 27) goes on to say: "Shortly after the 9/11 attacks, American began torturing prisoners, and they have never really stopped. However much these words have about them the ring of accusation, they must by now be accepted as fact. From Red Cross reports, Maj. Gen. Antonio M. Taguba's inquiry, James R. Schlesinger's Pentagon-sanctioned commission and other government and independent investigations, we have in our possession hundreds of accounts of 'cruel, inhuman and degrading' treatment – to use a phrase of the Red Cross – 'tantamount to torture.'"

The seriousness of this issue is highlighted by a review of the actual practice of torture. What is argued to be justified in individual cases has time and time again become widespread and indiscriminate. Among the best collections of the available documents, including memos from high level Bush administration officials redefining torture so narrowly as to make it ostensibly something else, see Danner, 2004. Another critical source of information and analysis on the legal policy of the Bush administration is the *American Journal of International Law*. Also see The National Security Archive web collection, "The Interrogation Documents: Debating U.S. Policy & Methods." http://www2.gwu.edu/~nsarchiv/NSAEBB/NSAEBB127/ See also Levinson, 2004b. See also Amnesty International, "United States of America: Human Dignity Denied, Torture & Accountability in the War on Terror," 2004. http://web.amnesty.org/library/Index/ENGAMR511452004 See also the Law of War Homepage (http://www.lawofwar.org/index.html) and especially the timeline and analysis of decisions by Judge Evan J. Wallach. http://lawofwar.org/Torture Memos_analysis.htm See also Greenberg & Dratel, 2005.

Finally, relevant here is Judith Herman's (1997) profound query: "Are there commonalities in the experiences of rape survivors and combat veterans, battered women and political prisoners, the survivors of vast concentration camps created by tyrants who rule nations, and the survivors of small, hidden concentration campus created by tyrants who rule in their homes?" Answering in the affirmative, Herman has brilliantly explored the common features of "complex post-traumatic stress disorder" affecting these various groups. For the first multi-disciplinary study of children and torture, which questions the current limiting of this terms to only those actions carried out by "public authorities," as defined in the relevant conventions, see van Buren, 1998.

extreme nature to rise to the level of torture. . . . Physical pain amounting to torture must be equivalent in intensity to the pain accompanying serious physical injury, such as organ failure, impairment of bodily function, or even death" (Levinson, 2004a: 5).[7]

So dramatic has been the Bush administration's view of the virtually unlimited sovereign powers of the President that well respected Constitutional scholar Carl Levinson (2004a: 8) argues that "the true *eminence grise* of the administration, particularly with regard to issues surround the possible propriety of torture," is none other than leading Nazi legal philosopher Carl Schmitt, Hitler's chief legal adviser, citing his famous statement: "There exists no norm that is applicable to chaos." Levinson (2004a: 9) goes on to warn of the ominous implications of "the articulation, on behalf of the Bush administration, of a view of presidential authority that is all too close to the power that Schmitt was willing to accord to his own Fuhrer."

As the time of this writing, it looks almost certain that one of the chief architects of Bush's torture policies – Chief Counsel Alberto Gonzales – will be approved as the next U.S. Attorney General, seen by many as his stepping stone to a Supreme Court appointment. In a series of memos in January 2002, Gonzales advised the President he had the constitutional authority to set aside the Geneva Conventions. In a January memo, Gonzales noted that among the "positive" benefits Gonzales saw flowing from this action was that it "Substantially reduces the threat of domestic criminal prosecution under the [1996] War Crimes Act (18 U.S.C. 2411) . . . [which] prohibits the commission of a "war crime," . . . defined to include any grave breach of GPW [Geneva Convention III on the Treatment of Prisoners of War]. . . . Punishments for violations of Section 2441 include the death penalty."[8]

Soon after Gonzales appeared at his confirmation hearing, the *New York Times* reported that the White House had successfully lobbied Congress to take out of recently passed intelligence legislation, language that would put new limits on extreme interrogation or torture by intelligence operatives. This same piece indicates that the coercive methods secretly approved by the Justice Department under the more narrow definition of torture cited above, were still considered legal even though this definition has ostensibly been changed.[9]

---

[7] I was first alerted to the Levinson piece in Chomsky, 2004.
[8] Cf. Gonzales (2002: 85); Office of the Attorney General (2002); Chomsky (2004: 4).
[9] New York Times, 1/13/05 and 1/19/05.

Numerous other examples could be given of U.S. violations of the Geneva Conventions, most especially the attack on Falluja General Hospital in November 2004, in defiance of Geneva's Article 19, which explicit prohibits attacks on or interference with medical facilities. The current conjuncture is thus one that has raised great concerns about the very future of liberal democracy in the U.S., as many see a real danger of fascism in the context of today's highly unstable international environment.

Indeed, a growing number of public officials, intellectuals and media outlets are increasingly promoting harsh interrogation methods and even torture as mechanisms to ostensibly stop the next terrorist attack against the U.S. A chorus of voices now argues that the next attacks inside the U.S., possibly involving nuclear weapons, may very well lead citizens to virtually demand "a national security state or permanent alert, with sealed borders, constant identity checks, and permanent detention camps for suspicious aliens and recalcitrant citizens" (Ignatieff, 2004: 153–154). That danger is indeed probably growing; yet the remedy is not to continue with the current U.S. policies but to change them radically and so minimize the ability of Al Qaeda and other groups to recruit for further terrorist attacks.

The Challenges Ahead in Historical Perspective

As the current practices of the Bush administration – with its disdain for international law – shows, changing current policies and practice will be no easy task. The international human rights movement has made many gains during this century and the codification of these norms in the form of law is an important achievement. That being said, there are still of course huge inequalities in the practice and application of international law, and it must be remembered too, that in recent years neoconservatives have sought to co-opt the international human rights movement by promoting war and humanitarian intervention as a solution to human rights abuses (Mandel 2004).[10]

Today, in the context of increased fear in the U.S. and widespread erroneously belief by the public that Iraq was involved in 9/11 and had weapons of mass destruction – a view consciously fostered by the Bush administration and their allies in the media – turning the tide will not be an easy task.

---

[10] On the history of the development of international humanitarian law, see Meron (1993, 1998a, b).

Indeed, in the United States, challenging the current de facto policy of torture will require a massive grassroots effort to educate people about the history of practices of torture, most especially the large body of empirical evidence about the degree to which torture, however narrowly justified at first, tends to become widespread and indiscriminate.[11] There were increased signs of just such grassroots activity around the Gonzales nomination by the Center for Constitutional Rights, the Torture Abolition and Survivors Support Coalition (TASSC), and related groups, though the full scale U.S. debate about torture necessary to stop this practice has yet to really take place.[12] If what is by now routine torture is to be stopped, there will have to be a campaign to educate people about the history of the practice, that at once critiques the morality of such activity and shows how it undermines security.

Indeed, in the present day, these horrific practices are arguably a chief method of new recruitment for terrorist groups like Al Qaeda. The fiftieth anniversary of the U.S. signing of all four of the Geneva conventions in July 1955 will be this coming July 2005 and might be a particularly poignant anniversary to aim at in raising awareness about this issue.

As if these tasks weren't enough, there is also the major task at hand to end the occupation of and human rights abuses in Iraq and hand over full and not fictive sovereignty to the Iraqi people. As important as this is, there are already rumblings about a possible future U.S. attack against Iran (Hersh, 2005). The larger task is to challenge the overall trajectory of current U.S. policy, which as Steven Rattner (2002: 913) rightly notes," "has endorsed an expansive view of its rights under *just ad* bellum, white insisting on a very narrow view of its obligations under *jus in bello*."

In light of the rather dire current context, it is however important to keep in mind as Noam Chomsky (2004) points out, how much has actually improved over the long term. Centuries ago, victims of European colonialism and their settler offshoots often elicited no sympathy, in sharp contrast to the demonstration of millions around the world against the invasion of Iraq, before the actual outbreak of war.

In addition, the September 11, 2001 terrorist attacks and the U.S. response has led to a revival of the global peace and anti-war movements, replete with the formation of a Global Anti-War Assembly, which has held numerous meetings across the globe, with one scheduled for the next World Social Forum

---

[11] Cf. Amnesty International (2004); Meisler (2005); Anderson (2005); Elkins (2005).
[12] See the important memoir of the current head of TASSC, Ortiz (2002).

in Porto Alegre Brazil in January 2005.[13] Among the particularly hopeful elements of these developments is that there appears to be increased collaboration between leading international non-governmental organizations, such as Focus on the Global South, the Transnational Institute – both of which focus on neoliberal globalization and related processes of militarization – and other groups around the globe. Moreover, the joining together of activists and scholars from the U.S, Western Europe, Asia, Latin America and Africa, and between the divides of North and South has been a real achievement.

Today, the development of both a more rigorous analysis and a program of action to tackle the intersection between neoliberal globalization and militarization and underscore its centrality in the global system, is among the more important issues facing the global movement for peace and social justice. U.S. and core military intervention has long played a key role in propping up the unequal structures of the global system in ways that increases U.S. profits and power at one and the same time.[14] The vastly increased U.S. military budget continues to serve as a critical mechanism for funding high technology industry, a hidden state industrial policy that allows for continued public subsidies for private profit in the U.S., practices which are denied for Third World states through institutions like the World Trade Organization. In addition, military spending serves increasingly to deflect demands for more resources to go to health, education, and human welfare, and thus plays an important role in class and electoral politics in the U.S.

Furthermore, "National Security" and militarization have also long been a key causal mechanism in environmental destruction and degradation (Dycus, 1996). And, as articulated by many of the leading figures in the field of human security and sustainable development, such as Mahbub Ul Haq (1995), Jean Dreze and Amartya Sen (2002: ch. 8), military spending is increasingly deleterious for democracy, undermining both military and human security, including by transferring much needed resources from sustainable development to the arms race and war. The issues listed above are but a few of the linkages

---

[13] See http://www.focusweb.org/main/html/Article540.html.

[14] In one of the more recent developments, the Pentagon is working on its own more advanced internet, the Global Information Grid (GIG), that aims to give "a God's-eye-view" of future battlefields; estimated to costs hundreds of billions of dollars, a new consortium formed in September 2004 to work on the project "includes an A-list of military contractors and technology power-houses: Boeing; Cisco Systems; Factiva, a joint venture of Dow Jones and Reuters; General Dynamics; Hewlett-Packard; Honeywell; I.B.M.; Lockheed Martin; Microsoft; Northrup Grumman; Oracle; Raytheon; and Sun Microsystems" (NYT, 11/25/04, A1, B2).

between the question of peace and social and environmental justice. A growing movement should target other areas of connection so as to sharpen the analysis and policy recommendations offered in the current conjuncture.

Yet if the intersection between neoliberal globalization and militarization is a key nexus to be focused on by the global peace and justice movements, doing so will take much work. For in the current environment, even though Anglo-American military policies and those of their adversaries increase global instability and militarization, activists and scholars must develop and press for real alternative security policies that address and reduce the threat of terrorism – state and non-state – without which it is unlikely that the funds so desperately needed for real sustainable development, based on meeting people's real human security needs will be met. Thus, articulating a common vision and program of action, that connects the dots among the movements and issues, remains one of the great challenge facing scholars and activists in the twenty-first century.

Author Biographical Statements

Jeffrey Ayres is an Associate Professor of Political Science at Saint Michael's College in Colchester, Vermont, USA. He is the author of *Defying Conventional Wisdom: Political Movements and Popular Contention Against North American Free Trade*, and other articles on globalization, social movements and transnational contention.

Gianpaolo Baiocchi writes on cities, politics, and social theory. His recent book on the Porto Alegre experiment, entitled *Militants and Citizens: the Politics of Participation in Porto Alegre*, is forthcoming in 2005.

Frederick Buttel made important contributions to rural sociology, environmental sociology, and the sociology of agriculture. He co-authored and edited several books including *Environment and Global Modernity* (2000), *Hungry for Profit: The Agribusiness Threat to Farmers, Food, and the Environment* (2000), and *Sociological Theory and the Environment: Classical Foundations, Contemporary Insights* (2002). He lost his long battle with cancer in 2005.

James Fenelon is the author of "Culturicide, Resistance and Survival of the Lakota 'Sioux Nation'" (Garland, 1998) and is completing a book with Thomas Hall "Indigenous Peoples and Globalization" (Johns Hopkins Press, forthcoming) James is Lakota/Dakota from Standing Rock Reservation, with works on Indian Identity, Sovereignty, Symbolic Racism and Indian Gaming, and current research activity on global Indigenous Struggles from a World Systems perspective.

Kenneth Gould is Professor of Sociology at St. Lawrence University. He writes on the political economy of environment, technology and development, examines social movement responses to environmental problems, the role of socio-economic inequality in environmental conflicts, and the impacts of economic globalization on efforts to achieve ecologically and socially sustainable development trajectories. He is co-author of *Environment and Society: The Enduring Conflict* (1994), and *Local Environmental Struggles* (1996).

Thomas Hall is Lester M. Jones Professor of Sociology at DePaul University in Greencastle, IN. In addition to researching indigenous peoples with James Fenelon, he is continuing work on a world-systems analysis of frontiers.

Tammy Lewis is the Chair of the Sociology and Anthropology Department at Muhlenberg College in Allentown, PA. She is a co-author, with Craig Humphrey and Fred Buttel, of *Environment, Energy and Society: A New Synthesis* (2002). She researches transnational environmentalism, with an emphasis on Latin America and the Caribbean.

Bruce Podobnik is Assistant Professor of Sociology at Lewis and Clark College. He is the author of *Global Energy Shifts* (2005), as well as articles on environmental and social movement topics.

Thomas Reifer is Assistant Professor of Sociology at the University of San Diego. He has published widely on U.S. intelligence, and on the relationship between neoliberal globalization, militarization, labor and peace and social justice movements. He edited the recent volume, *Globalization, Hegemony and Power* (2004).

J. Timmons Roberts is Professor of Sociology and Director of Environmental Science and Policy at the College of William and Mary. He is author of *Chronicles from the Environmental Justice Frontline* (2001), *Trouble in Paradise* (2003), and is currently completing a book with Ken Gould and Tammy Lewis on Blue-Green coalitions.

Robert Ross is Professor of Sociology at Clark University where he directs the International Studies Stream. He is the author of *Slaves to Fashion: Poverty and Abuse in the New Sweatshops* (2004) and was a national officer of Students for A Democratic Society.

Jackie Smith is associate professor of sociology and peace studies at the Joan B. Kroc Institute for International Peace Studies at the University of Notre Dame. She has co-edited three books on transnational social movements, including *Transnational Social Movements and Global Politics* (1997), *Globalization and Resistance: Transnational Dimensions of Social Movements* (2002), and *Coalitions Across Borders: Transnational Protest and the Neoliberal Order* (2004). She has published more than thirty articles in books and journals such as *American Sociological Review, Social Forces, Mobilization,* and *International Sociology.*

Lesley Wood is Assistant Professor of Sociology at York University. Her interests and publications are in the area of globalization and social movements.

Bibliography

Abers, Rebecca. 2000. Inventing local democracy: grassroots politics in Brazil. Boulder: Lynne Rienner Publishers.

Ackerman, Seth (2001). "Prattle in Seattle: Media Coverage Misrepresented the Protest," Pp. 48–52 in Globalize This!: The Battle Against the World Trade Organization and Corporate Rule, edited by K. Danaher and R. Burbach. Monroe, ME: Common Courage Press.

Acuna, Carlos and William Smith. 1994. "The Political Economy of Structural Adjustment: The Logic of Support and Opposition to Neoliberal Reform," in William Smith, Carlos Acuna and Eduardo Gamarra, eds. Latin American Political Economy in the Age of Neoliberal Reform: Theoretical and Comparative Perspecives for the 1990s. Boulder, CO: Lynne Rienner.

Adamovsky, Ezequiel. 2003. "Another Forum is Possible; Whose Bridges are We Building' Do We Need a New International?" http://www.nadir.org/nadir/initiativ/agp/free/wsf/anotherforum.htm

AFL-CIO. 2003. "Iraq". Executive Council Actions.

Coughlin, Ginny. 2002 (May 14). 1997. Interviews.

Aldrich, George, "Editorial Comments: The Taliban, Al Qaeda, & the Determination of Illegal Combatants," American Journal of International Law, October 2002, Vol. 96, #4, pp. 891–898.

American Journal of International Law, various issues.

Amin, Samir. 2002. "The Priority of Strengthening Social Movements on a Global Scale," pp. 45–55 in: Leena Rikkila and Katarina Patomaki (eds.). From a Global Market Place to Political Spaces, Helsinki, Finland: Network Institute for Global Democratization.

Amin, Samir, Andre Gunder-Frank, Immanuel Wallerstein. 1990. Transforming the Revolution: Social Movements and the World System. New York: Monthly Review Press.

Amnesty International, "United States of America: Human Dignity Denied, Torture & Accountability in the War on Terror," 2004.

Ancelovici, Marcos. 2002. "Organizing Against Globalization: The Case of ATTAC in France." Politics and Society 30(3): 427–463.

Anderson, David, Histories of the Hanged: The Dirty War in Kenya & the End of Empire, New York: W.W. Norton, 2005.

Anderson-Sherman, Arnold and Doug McAdam. 1982. "American Black Insurgency and the World Economy: A Political Process Model." Pp. 165–188 in Ascent and Decline in the World System, edited by E. Friedman. Beverly Hills: Sage.

Araghi, F. (2000). "The Great Global Enclosure of Our Times: Peasants and the Agrarian Question at the End of the Twentieth Century." Pp. 145–160 in Hungry For Profit, edited by F. Magdoff. New York: Monthly Review Press.

Aufheben. 2001. "'Anti-Capitalism' as Ideology . . . and as Movement?," Aufheben, 10, pp. 1–3.

Ayres, Jeffrey. 1998. Defying Conventional Wisdom: Political Movements and Popular Contention Against North American Free Trade. Toronto: University of Toronto Press.

Ayres, Jeffrey and Sidney Tarrow. 2002. "The Shifting Grounds for Transnational Civic Activity," in After September 11: Perspectives from the Social Sciences.

Baiocchi, Gianpaolo. 2002. "Synergizing Civil Society; State-Civil Society Regimes and Democratic Decentralization in Porto Alegre, Brazil." Political Power and Social Theory 15:3–86.

Bello, Walden. (2001). "UNCTAD: Time to Lead, Time to Challenge the WTO," in Globalize This!: The Battle Against the World Trade Organization and Corporate Rule, edited by K. Danaher and R. Burbach. Monroe, ME: Common Courage Press.

Bello, Walden. 2002. "Battling Barbarism." Foreign Policy. 132:41–42.

Benford, Robert and David Snow. 2000. "Framing Processes and Social Movements: an Overview and Assessment." Annual Review of Sociology.

Bennholdt-Thomsen, Veronika, Nicholas Fraclas, Claudia Von Werlhof. 2001. There Is an Alternative: Subsistence and Worldwide Resistance to Corporate Globalization. London: Zed Books.

Beozzo, Jos' Oscar, and Apolo Heringer Lisboa. 1983. "PT: avalia' 'o eleitoral." Vozes 77:18–36.

Bergquist, Charles. 1986. Labor in Latin America: Comparative Essays on Chile, Argentina, Venezuela, and Colombia. Stanford, CA: Stanford University Press.

Bidwai, Praful. (2003). "A Great Movement is Born." Canadian Dimension.

Biolsi, Thomas. 1995. "Bringing the Law Back In: Legal Rights and the Regulation of Indian-White Relations on the Rosebud Reservation." Current Anthropology 36:4 (Aug.-Oct.): 543–571.

Blackfire. 2001. One Nation Under, Canyon Records.

Bob, Clifford. 2001. "Marketing Rebellion: Insurgent Groups, International Media, and NGO Support." International Politics 38:311–334.

Bodley, John H. 2003. Power of Scale: A Global History Approach. Armonk, NY: ME Sharpe.

Boli, John and George Thomas. 1997. "World Culture in the World Polity: A Century of Non-Governmental Organization." American Sociological Review 62:171–190.

Boli, John and George M. Thomas, ed. 1999. Constructing World Culture: International Nongovernmental Organizations Since 1875. Stanford:Stanford University Press.

Boswell, Terry and Christopher Chase-Dunn. 2000. The Spiral of Capitalism and Socialism: The Decline of State Socialism and the Future of the World-System. Boulder, CO: Lynne-Rienner.

Boyer, Paul. 1997. Native American Colleges: Progress and Prospects. An Ernest L. Boyer Project of the Carnegie Foundation for the Advancement of Teaching. Princeton, NJ: Carnegie Foundation for the Advancement of Teaching.

Brecher, J.T. Costello and B. Smith (2000). Globalization From Below: The Power of Solidarity. Boston: South End Press.

Broad, Robin and John Cavanagh. 1999. "The Death of the Washington Consensus?" World Policy Journal 16(3): 79–87.

Brown, Phil and Edwin Mikkelsen. 1990. No Safe Place: Toxic Waste, Leukemia, and Community Action. Berkeley: University of California Press.

Brown, Kaye. 1976. "Quantitative Testing and Revitalization Behavior: On Carroll's Explanation of the Ghost Dance." American Sociological Review 41(August): 740–744.

Brulle, R. (2000). Agency, Democracy, and Nature: The U.S. Environmental Movement from a Critical Theory Perspective. MIT Press: Cambridge, MA.

Bryant, Bunyan and Mohai, Paul. eds. 1992. Race and the Incidence of Environmental Hazards: A Time for Discourse. San Francisco: Westview Press.

Brysk, Allison. 1996. "Turning Weakness Into Strength: The Internationalization of Indian Rights." Latin American Perspectives 23:38–58.

Brysk, Alison. 2000. From Tribal Village to Global Village: Indigenous Peoples Struggles in Latin America. Stanford: Stanford University Press.

Bullard, Robert. 1990. Dumping in Dixie: Race, Class, and Environmental Quality. Boulder: Westview.

Bullard, Robert. (1993). Confronting Environmental Racism: Voices from the Grass Roots. Boston: South End Press.

Burke, Jason, Al Qaeda: The True Story of Radical Islam, London: I.B. Taurus, 2004.

Burmeister, L., J.-C. Jao, and K. Sakamoto. (2001). "The Multifunctionality Challenge to the WTO Regime," Paper presented at the annual meeting of the American Sociological Association, Anaheim, CA., August.

Cadwalader, Sandra D. and Vine Deloria (eds). 1984. The Aggressions of Civilization: Federal Indian Policy since the 1880's. Philadelphia: Temple University Press.

Carter and Barringer. 2001. "In Patriotic Times, Dissent is Muted." The New York Times. 7 December.

Cassen, Bernard. 2002. "On the ATTAC." New Left Review: 41–61.

Cattani, Antonio David (ed.). 2001. F'rum Social Mundial: A Constru' 'o de Um Mundo Melhor. Porto Alegre, Brazil: Editora Vozes.

Chabot, Sean and Jan Willem Duyvendak. 2002. "Globalization and transnational diffusion between social movements" Theory and Society 31:697–740, 2002.

Chabot, Sean. 2000. "Transnational Diffusion and the African American Reinvention of the Gandhian Repertoire." Mobilization 5(2): 201–216.

Champagne, Duane. 2005. "Rethinking Native Relations with Contemporary Nation-States," pp. 1–1 – 1–33 in Indigenous People and the Modern State, edited by Duane Champagne, Karen Torjesen, and Susan Steiner. Walnut Creek, CA: AltaMira Press.

Champagne, Duane. 2003. "Indigenous Strategies for Engaging Globalism." Pp. xix–xxxii in The Future of Indigenous Peoples: Strategies for Survival and Development, edited by Duane Champagne and Imael Abu-Saad. Los Angeles: UCLA American Indian Studies Center.

Chase-Dunn, Christopher and Thomas D. Hall. 1997. Rise and Demise: Comparing World-Systems. Boulder: Westview Press.

Chase-Dunn, Christopher, Yukio Kawano, and Benjamin Brewer. 2000. "Trade Globalization Since 1795: Waves of Integration in the World-System," American Sociological Review, 65, pp. 77–95.

Chomksy, Noam, "Imperial Presidency," Znet, December 17, 2004.

Clark, John. 2003. Worlds Apart: Civil Society and the Battle for Ethical Globalization. Bloomfield, CT: Kumarian Press.

Clark, Robert. 2002. Global Awareness: Thinking Systematically About the World. Lanham, MD: Rowman & Littlefield.

Clastres, Pierre. 1980. The Archaeology of Violence. New York: Semiotext(e).

Cohen, R., and S.M. Rai (eds.) (2000). Global Social Movements. London: Ahtlone Press.

Collier, George A. 1999. Basta!: Land & the Zapatista Rebellion in Chiapas. Oakland, CA: Food First Books.

Cole, Luke W. and Sheila R. Foster. 2002. "From the Ground Up: Environmental Racism and the Rise of the Environmental Justice Movement." New York: NYU Press.

Cooper, Frederick. 1996. Decolonization and African Society: The Labor Question in French and British Africa. Cambridge: Cambridge University Press.

Cooper, Marc. 2002. "From Protest to Politics: A Report from Porto Alegre." The Nation. 11 March: 11–16.

Couto, Claudio Goncalves. 1994. "Mudanca e Crise: O PT no Governo de Sao Paulo." Luan Nova: 145–164.

Crossley, N. (2002). "Global Anti-Corporate Struggle: A Preliminary Analysis," British Journal of Sociology. 53:667–691.

Cullen, Pauline. 2003. "European NGOs and EU-Level Mobilization for Social Rights." Doctoral dissertation Thesis, Sociology, SUNY- Stony Brook, Stony Brook, NY.

Danaher, K. (ed.) (2001). Democratizing the Global Economy: The Battle Against the World Bank and the IMF. Monroe, ME: Common Courage Press.

Danaher, Kevin and Roger Burbach. 2000. Globalize This! The Battle Against the World Trade Organization and Corporate Rule. Monroe, ME: Common Courage Press.

Danner, Mark, Torture & Truth: America, Abu Ghraib, & the War on Terror, New York: New York Review of Books, 2004.

Danner, Mark, "We Are All Torturers Now," New York Times, January 6, 2005, A27.

Debray, Regis. 1967. Revolution in the Revolution. New York, NY: Grove Press.

della Porta, Donatella and Hanspeter Kriesi. 1999. "Social Movements in a Globalizing World: An Introduction." Pp. 3–23 in Social Movements in a Globalizing World, edited by D. della Porta, H. Kriesi, and D. Rucht. New York: St. Martin's Press.

Della Porta, Donnatella and Sidney Tarrow. 2002. "After Genoa: the Anti-Global Movement, the Police and Transnational Politics." Items: Social Science Research Council.

Deloria, Vine Jr. and Wilkins, David E. 2000. Tribes, Treaties, and Constitutional Tribulations. Austin: University of Texas Press.

Deloria, Jr. Vine. & Lytle, Clifford. 1984. The Nations within, the past and future of American Indian sovereignty. New York: Pantheon Books.

Directorate General for Research. 1998. An Appraisal of Technologies of Political Control. Luxembourg: European Parliament.

Dowie, Mark. (1995). Losing Ground: American Environmentalism at the Close of the Twentieth Century. Cambridge, MA: MIT Press.

Dreze, Jean & Amartya Sen, India: Development & Participation, New York: Oxford University Press, 2002.

Drohan, Madelaine. 2003. "WTO Talks: We are Risking a Collapse," Toronto Globe and Mail 29 July.

Dunaway, Wilma. 2003a. "Has Terroism Changed the World-System Forever?" Pp. 3–13 in Emerging Issues in the 21st Century World-System: Vol. I: Crises and Resistance in the 21st World-System, edited by Wilma A. Dunaway. Westport, CT: Praeger.

Dunaway, Wilma. 2003b. Dunaway, Wilma A. 2003. "Ethnic Conflict in the Modern World-System: The Dialectics of Counter-Hegemonic Resistance in an Age of Transition." Journal of World-Systems Research 9:1 (Winter): 3–34.

Dunkley, G. (2000). The Free Trade Adventure. London: Zed Books.

Dycus, Stephen, National Defense & the Environment, Hanover: University Press of New England, 1996.

Elkins, Caroline, Imperial Reckoning: The Untold Story of Britain's Gulag in Kenya, New York: Henry Holt, 2005.

Elliott, Kimberly Ann and Richard B. Freeman. 2000. "White Hats Or Don Quixotes? Human Rights Vigilantes In The Global Economy." National Bureau of Economic Research.

Ellis-Jones, Mark. 2003. States of Unrest III. World Development Movement.

Epstein, B. (2001). "Anarchism and the Anti-corporate globalization Movement," Monthly Review. 53.

Erlanger, Steve. 2001. "Italy's Premier Calls Western Civilization Superior to Islamic World." The New York Times. 27 September.

Estabrook, Thomas, Carlos Eduardo Siqueira, and Eduardo Paes Macado. 2000. "Labor-Community Alliances in Petrochemical Regions in the United States and Brazil: What Does It Take to Win." Capitalism Nature Socialism September: 113–145.

Evangelista, Matthew. 1995. "The Paradox of State Strength: Transnational Relations, Domestic Structures and Security Policy in Russia and the Soviet Union." International Organization 49:1–38.

Ewald, Shawn. 2002. "Coming off the Fence: A20 Quebec City," SchNews of the World (301), pp. 1–2.

Faux, Jeff. 2003. "A Tale of Two Cities: Davos and Porto Alegre Square off on the Global Economy." The American Prospect. 14(2): 13–15.

Featherstone , Liza. 2002 (May 13). "Strange Marchfellows. The Nation.

Fenelon, James. 2000. "Traditional and Modern Perspectives on Indian Gaming: The Struggle for Sovereignty." Pp. 108–128 in Indian Gaming: Who Wins?, edited by Angela Mullis and David Kamper. Los Angeles: Native American Studies.

Fenelon, James. 1998. Culturicide, Resistance, and Survival of the Lakota (Sioux Nation). New York: Garland Publishing.

Fenelon, James V. 1997. "From Peripheral Domination to Internal Colonialism: Socio-Political Change of the Lakota on Standing Rock." Journal of World-Systems Research 3:2 (Spring): 259–320. [http://jwsr.ucr.edu/index.php].

Fenelon, James. 2002. "Dual Sovereignty of Native Nations, the United States, & Traditionalists." Humboldt Journal of Social Relations 27:1: 106–145.

Finnemore, Martha. 1996. National Interests in International Society. Ithaca, NY: Cornell University Press.

Fisher, William, and Thomas Ponniah (Eds.). 2003. Another World is Possible: Popular Alternatives to Globalization at the World Social Forum. London: Zed.

Fisk, Robert. 2001 (December 10). "My beating by refugees is a symbol of the hatred and fury of this filthy war." The Independent.

Flacks, R., "The Liberated Generation: Social Psychological Roots of Student Protest", Journal of Social Issues, (23:52–75), 1967.

Flacks, R., Youth and Social Change. Chicago: Rand McNally, 1971.

Foster, John Bellamy. 1999. The Vulnerable Planet: A Short Economic History of the Environment. New York: Monthly Review Press.

Fox, Jonathan and L. David Brown. 1998. The Struggle for Accountability: The World Bank, NGOs, and Grassroots Movements. Cambridge: MIT Press.

Friedman, Elisabeth Jay, Ann Marie Clark, and Kathryn Hochstetler. Forthcoming. The Sovereign Limits of Global Civil Society.

Friedman, Thomas. 2000. The Lexis and the Olive Tree: Understanding Globalization. New York, NY: Anchor Books.

Friedman, Thomas. 1999. "Senseless in Seattle." The New York Times. 1 December.

Fries, Jacob. 2002. "Anarchists Discover an Image Problem." The New York Times. 28 January.

Garcia, Marco Aur'lio. 1991. "'Socialdemocracia o comunismo"' Nueva Sociedad 114.

Hardt, Michael. 2002. "Today's Badung'" New Left Review: 112–118.

Gedicks, Al. 2001. Resource Rebels: Native Challenges to Mining and Oil Corporations. Cambridge, MA: South End Press.

Gedicks, Al. 1993. The New Resource Wars: Native and Environmental Struggles Against Multinational Corporations. Boston, MA: South End Press.

Geneva Conventions. http://www.redcross.org.uk/index.asp?id=11

George, S., G. Monbiot, L. German, T. Hayter, A. Callinicos and K. Moody (2001). Anti-Capitalism: A Guide to the Movement. London: Bookmarks.

Gerner, Deborah, Philip Schrodt, Ronald Francisco, & Judith Weddle. 1994. "Machine Coding of Event Data Using Regional and International Sources," International Studies Quarterly, 38, pp. 91–119.

Geyer, Robert and Jeffrey Ayres. 1995. "Rethinking Conventional Wisdom: Political Opposition Towards Integration in Canada and Denmark." Journal of Commonwealth and Comparative Politics. 31(3): 377–99.

Girvan, Norman. 1976. Corporate Imperialism: Conflict and Expropriation: Transnational Corporations and Economic Nationalism in the Third World. New York, NY: Monthly Review Press.

Gonzales, Alberto, "Memorandum for the President," January 25, 2002, in Mark Danner, Torture & Truth: America, Abu Ghraib, & the War on Terror, New York: New York Review of Books, 2004, pp. 83–87.

Gould, K., T. Lewis and J.T. Roberts (2004). "Blue-Green Coalitions: Constraints and Possibilities in the Post 9–11 Political Environment." Journal of World Systems Research X (1): 91–118.

Gould, Kenneth A.; Schnaiberg, Allan, and Weinberg, Adam S. 1996. Local Environmental Struggles: Citizen Activism in the Treadmill of Production. Cambridge: Cambridge University Press.

Greenberg, Karen J. & Joshua L. Dratel, ed., The Torture Papers: The Road to Abu Ghraib, Cambridge University Press, 2005.

Grundy, John and Alison Howell. 2001. "Negotiating the Culture of Resistance: A Critical Assessment of Protest Politics," Studies in Political Economy 66: 121–132.

Guidry, John A., Michael D. Kennedy, and Mayer N. Zald. forthcoming. "Globalizations and Social Movements." Chapter 1 in Introduction: Globalizations and Social Movements, edited by J.A. Guidry, M.D. Kennedy, and M.N. Zald.

Habermas, Jurgen. 2001. "Why Europe Needs a New Constitution." New Left Review. 11:5–26.

Hall, Thomas D. and James V. Fenelon. 2003. Indigenous Resistance to Globalization: What Does the Future Hold?, 2003. Pp. 173–188 in Emerging Issues in the 21st Century World-System: Vol. I: Crises and Resistance in the 21st World-System, edited by Wilma A. Dunaway. Westport, CT: Praeger.

Hall, Thomas D. and Joane Nagel. 2000. "Indigenous Peoples." Pp. 1295–1301 in The Encyclopedia of Sociology, Vol. 2, revised edition, edited by Edgar F. Borgatta and Rhonda J.V. Montgomery. New York: Macmillan Reference.

Hall, Thomas. 2002. "World-Systems, Frontiers, and Ethnogenesis: Incorporation and Resistance to State Expansion." Pp. 35–66 in Borderlines in A Globalized World. Edited by Gerhard Preyer and Mathias Bos. Dordrecht, Boston, London: Kluwer Academic Publishers.

Hall, Thomas D. and James Fenelon. in press a. Indigenous Peoples and Globalization: Resistance and Revitalization in World-Systems Analysis. Baltimore: Johns Hopkins University Press.

Hall, Thomas D. and James V. Fenelon. in press b. "Indigenous Peoples and Hegemonic Change: Threats to Sovereignty or Opportunities for Resistance?" Forthcoming in Hegemonic Decline: Past and Present, edited by Jonathan Friedmand and Christopher Chase-Dunn. Boulder: Paradigm Press.

Hannan, Maichael T. and John Freeman. 1977. "The Population Ecology of Organizations." American Journal of Sociology 82:929–64.

Hardt, Michael, and Antonio Negri. 2000. Empire. Cambridge, Mass.: Harvard University Press.

Harnecker, Marta. 1994. El Sue'o era Posible. Santiago, Chile: Lom Ediciones.

Harvey, David. 1989. The Condition of Postmodernity: An Enquiry into the Origins of Cultural Change. London: Basil Blackwell.

Hathaway, Will and David S. Meyer. 1993–4. "Competition and Cooperation in Social Movement Coalitions: Lobbying for Peace in the 1980s. Berkeley Journal of Sociology 38:157–183.

Henderson, Hazel. 1999. Beyond Globalization: Shaping a Sustainable Global Economy. West Hartford, CT: Kumarian Press.

Herman, Judith Lewis, Trauma and Recovery: The Aftermath of Violence-From Domestic Abuse to Political Terror, New York: Basic Books, 1997.

Hersh, Seymour M., "The Coming Wars," Annals of National Security, NewYorker, January 17, 2005.

Hoerner, J. Andrew and Barry Phelps. 2002. "A Working Environment: Addressing

Climate Change While Protecting Workers and the Economy." Environmental Protection 13(6): 36. http:// www.sustainableeconomy.org accessed on 7 August 2002.

Holly, Derill. 2004. "Groups plan demonstrations for financial institutions' annual spring meetings," April 8, 2004, American Press.

Horton, Scott, "A Nuremberg Lesson," Los Angeles Times, Thursday, January 20, 2005, p. B13.

Hovey, Michael. 1997. "Interceding at the United Nations: The Right of Conscientious Objection." in Transnational Social Movements and Global Politics: Solidarity Beyond the State, edited by J. Smith, C. Chatfield, and R. Pagnucco. Syracuse, NY: Syracuse University Press.

Huber, Emily and Jamie McCallum, "Anti-Globalization, Pro-Peace?" Mother Jones, 17 October 2001.

Hurley, Andrew. 1995. Environmental Inequalities: Class, Race, and Industrial Pollution in Gary, Indiana, 1945–1980. Chapel Hill: University of North Carolina Press.

Ignatieff, Michael, The Lesser Evil: Political Ethics in an Age of Terror, Columbia University Press, 2004.

Imig, Doug. 2001. "Building a Transnational Archive of Contentious Events," pp. 253–259 in: Doug Imig & Sidney Tarrow (Eds.) Contentious Europeans: Protest and Politics in an Emerging Polity. Lanham: Rowman & Littlefield Publishers, Inc.

Indy Media (Seattle), & Big Noise Films. 2000. This is What Democracy Looks Like. Seattle, WA: Big Noise Films.

Indymedia Italia. 2001. "Genoa G8: What Happened?," Indymedia Italia, July 2001.

Institute For Social Research. 2001 (October 9). "How America Responds to Terrorist Attacks" (Parts 1 and 2).

Iverson, Peter. 1999. "We Are Still Here": American Indians in the Twentieth Century. Wheeling, IL: Harlan Davidson.

Jacobi, Pedro. 1995. "Alcances y Limites de Gobiernos Progresistas en Brasil." Revista Mexicana de Sociologia 57:143–162.

Jeffress, Lynn. 2001. "A World Struggle is Underway: An Interview with Jose Bove," Z Magazine, June, pp. 1–3.

Jinks, Dere, "The Declining Significance of POW Status," Harvard International Law Journal, Volume 45, Number 2, Summer 2004, pp. 367–442.

Jinks, Derek & David Sloss, "Is the President Bound By the Geneva Conventions?," Cornell Law Review, Volume 90, #1, November 2004, pp. 97–202.

Jinks, Derek, "September 11 and the Laws of War," Yale Journal of International Law 28, 2003, pp. 1–49.

Jorgensen, Joseph J. 1972. The Sun Dance Religion: Power for the Powerless. Chicago: University of Chicago Press.

Just Transition Alliance. 2002. "Local Projects. http://www.jtalliance.org/docs/projects.htm.

Katzenberger, Elaine, ed. 1995. First World, Ha Ha Ha!: The Zapatista Challenge. San Francisco: City Lights Books.

Kazis, Richard & Grossman, Richard L. 1991. Fear at Work: Job Blackmail, Labor and the Environment. Philadelphia: New Society Publishers.

Keck, Margaret. 1992. The Worker's Party and Democratization in Brazil. New Haven: Yale University Press.

Keck, Margaret. 1998. "Environmental Advocacy Networks." Pp. 121–163 in Activists Beyond Borders, edited by M.E. Keck and K. Sikkink. Ithaca: Cornell University Press.

Keck, Margaret, and Kathryn Sikkink. 1998. Activists Beyond Borders: Advocacy Networks in International Politics. Ithaca, NY: Cornell University Press.

Khagram, Sanjeev, James V. Riker and Kathryn Sikkink. 2002. Restructuring World Politics: Transnational Social Movements, Networks, and Norms. Minneapolis: University of Minnesota Press.

Klandermans, Bert et al. 1999. "Injustice and Adversarial Frames in a Supranational Political Context: Farmers' Protest in the Netherlands and Spain," pp. 134–47 in Donatella della Porta, Hanspeter Kriesi and Dieter Rucht, eds. 1999. Social Movements in a Globalizing World. New York: St. Martin's Press.

Klein, Naomi. 2000. No Logo: Taking Aim at the Brand Bullies. Picador.

Klein, Naomi. 2003. "The Hijacking of the World Social Forum." Accessed on: May 1, 2003. http://www.nadir.org/nadir/initiativ/agp/free/wsf/naomiklein.htm

Klein, Naomi. 2001. "Farewell to 'the End of History'" Organization and Vision in Anti-Corporate Movements," pp. 1–14 in Leo Panitch and Colin Leys, eds., Socialist Register 2002: A World of Contradictions. London: Merlin Press.

Klein, Naomi (October 10, 2001). Protesting in the Post-WTC Age The Nation. Viewed on October 15, 2001 http://www.alternet.org/story.html?StoryID=11684

Klein, Naomi. 1999. "Rebels in Search of Rules." The New York Times. 2 December.

Know Your Rights. 2004. Know Your Rights Resources. New York, NY: National Lawyers Guild.

Korzeniewicz, Robert and Timothy Moran. 1997. "World-Economic Trends in the Distribution of Income 1965–1992." American Journal of Sociology 102:1000–1039.

Korzeniewicz, Roberto and William Smith. 2001. "Protest and Collaboration: Transnational Civil Society Networks and the Politics of Summitry and Free Trade in the Americas." Agenda Paper 51. North-South Center. University of Miami.

Kreider, Aaron. 2000 (August 7). "Privilege and our movement." Messages posted to usas@listbot.com.

Kreider, Aaron. 2002 (April 9). "USAS affiliates." Message posted to usas@-yahoogroups.com.

Kriesberg, Louis. 1997. "Social Movements and Global Transformation." Pp. 3–18 in Transnational Social Movements and World Politics: Solidarity Beyond the State, edited by J. Smith, C. Chatfield, and R. Pagnucco. Syracuse, NY: Syracuse University Press.

Kumar. 1992. Raising Up a Prophet: The African-American Encounter with Gandhi. Boston: Beacon Press.

LacLau, Ernesto, & Chantal Mouffe. 1985. Hegemony and Socialist Strategy. London: Verso.

Law of War Homepage. http://www.lawofwar.org/index.html

Laxer, Gordon. 2003. "Stop Rejecting Sovereignty." Canadian Dimension. Jan./Feb.

LeClerc, Patrice and Kenneth A. Gould. 2003. "USA PATRIOT Act: Why We All Should Be Terrified." Socialist Studies Bulletin (71).

Levine, Adeline G. 1982. Love Canal: Science, Politics and People. Lexington, MA: D.C. Heath and Company.

Levinson, Sanford, "Torture in Iraq & the Rule of Law in America," Daedalus: Journal of the American Academy of the Arts & Sciences, Summer 2004a, pp. 5–9.

Levinson, Sanford, ed., Torture, New York: Oxford University Press, 2004b.

Lipset, Seymour Martin. 1997. "The Iron Law of Oligarchy." Pp. 385–392 in Social Movements: Perspectives and Issues, edited by Steven Buechler and F. Kurt Cylke jr. New York: Mayfield Publishing.

Los Angeles Times, "Geneva Convention Overhaul Considered," Peter Wallsten, January 7, 2005, p. A24.

Lowy, Michael. 1987. "A New Type of Party: The Brazilian PT." Latin American Perspectives 14:453–464.

Lubeck Paul M. and Thomas E. Reifer, "The Politics of Global Islam: US Hegemony,

Globalization and Islamist Social Movements," in Thomas E. Reifer, ed., Globalization, Hegemony & Power: Antisystemic Movements and the Global System, Boulder, Co: Paradigm Publishers, 2004, pp. 162–180.

Madley, J. (2000). Hungry for Trade. London: Zed Books.

Maiba, Hermann. 2001. "Transnational Grassroots Mobilization Against Globalization," Paper presented at the American Sociological Association Annual Meeting, Anaheim, CA.

Mandel, Michael, How America Gets Away With Murder: Illegal Wars, Collateral Damage & Crimes Against Humanity, London: Pluto Press, 2004.

Maney, Gregory M. 2002. "Transnational Structures and Protest: Linking Theories and Assessing Evidence." Pp. 31–50 in Globalization and Resistance: Transnational Dimensions of Social Movements, edited by J. Smith and H. Johnston. Lanham, Md.: Rowman & Littlefield.

Mankoff, Milton and Flacks, Richard. 1971. "The Changing Social Base Of The American Student Movement". The Annals of the American Academy of Political and Social Science 395:55–67.

Markoff, John. 1996. Waves of Democracy: Social Movements and Political Change. Thousand Oaks: Pine Forge Press.

Markoff, John. 1999. "Globalization and the Future of Democracy." Journal of World-Systems Research http://csf.colorado.edu/wsystems/jwsr.html 5:242–262.

Marymount University Center for Ethical Concerns. 1999. "The Consumers and Sweatshops".

Massicotte, Marie-Josée. 2003. "Local Organizing and Global Struggles: Coalition-Building for Social Justice in the Americas." Pp. 105–125 in Gordon Laxer and Sandra Halperin (eds). Global Civil Society and Its Limits (Basinstoke, UK: Palgrave).

McAdam, Doug. John McCarthy and Mayer Zald. 1988. "Social Movements," in Neil Smelser ed. Handbook of Sociology. Newbury Park, CA: Sage: 695–738.

McAdam, Doug, Sidney Tarrow and Charles Tilly. 2001. Dynamics of Contention. Cambridge University Press.

McAdam, Doug. 1982. The Political Process and the Development of Black Insurgency. Chicago: University of Chicago Press.

McAdam, Doug and Dieter Rucht. 1993. "The Cross-National Diffusion of Movement Ideas." The Annals of the American Academy of Political and Social Science 528:56–74.

McAdam, Doug. 1982. Political Process and the Development of Black Insurgency, 1930–1970. Chicago.

McCarthy, John D. 1997. "The Globalization of Social Movement Theory." in Transnational Social Movements and Global Politics: Solidarity Beyond the State. Edited by Jackie Smith et al., Syracuse, N.Y.: Syracuse University Press.

McLeod, Leonard, producer. 2001. In the Light of Reverence: Protecting America's Sacred Lands. Oley, PA: Bullfrog Films.

McMichael, Philip. 2003. Development and Social Change: A Global Perspective, 3rd ed. Thousand Oaks, CA: Pine Forge Press.

Meisler, Stanley, "A Familiar Tale of Uprising and Bloody Supression," L.A. Times, Sunday, January 16, 2005, p. R5.

Meneguello, Rachel. 1989. PT: A Forma' 'o de Um Partido 1979–1982. Rio de Janeiro, Brazil: Editora Paz e Terra.

Meron, Theodor, Henry's Wars & Shakespeare's Laws: Perspectives on the Law of War in the Later Middle Ages, New York: Oxford, 1993.

Meron, Theodor. 1998. War Crimes Law Comes of Age, New York: Oxford.

Meron, Theodor. 1998. Bloody Constraint: War & Chivarly in Shakespeare, New York: Oxford.

Miami Activist Defense. 2003. "Miami Mayor Diaz's 'Model for Homeland Defense' Equals Suspension of the Constitution," STOPFTAA (Press Release).

Michaelson, Marc. 1994. "Wangari Maathai and Kenya's Green Belt Movement: Exploring the Evolution and Potentialities of Consensus Movement Mobilization." Social Problems 41:540–561.

Midnight Notes. 2001. Auroras of the Zapatistas. Brooklyn, NY: Autonomedia.

Minchin, Timothy J. 2003. Forging a Common Bond: Labor and Environmental Quality. Boulder: Westview.

Minkoff, Deborah. 1995. Organizing for Equality: the Evolution of Women's and Racial Ethnic Organizations in America, 1955–1985. New Brunswick, NJ: Rutgers University Press.

Mische, Ann. 2003. "Cross-talk in Movements: Reconceiving the Culture-Network Link," in Mario Diani and Doug McAdam (eds.), Social Movements and Networks. Oxford and New York: Oxford University Press.

Moberg, David. 1999. "Brothers and Sisters Greens and Labor: it's a coalition that gives corporate polluters fits." Sierra (January/February). http://www.justtransition.org/articles-greens-labor.htm accessed on 5 August 2002.

Monks, John and John Sweeney. 2003. (January 30). Letter to Prime Minister Blair and President Bush.

Mullis, Angela and David Kamper. 2000 Indian Gaming: Who Wins? Los Angeles: Native American Studies.

Murphy, Gillian Hughs. 2002. "A Double-Edged Sword: Coalitions and the Development of the Global Environmental Movement." M.A. Thesis, Sociology, University of Washington, Seattle.

Nagel, Joane. 1996. American Indian Ethnic Renewal: Red Power and the Resurgence of Identity and Culture. Oxford University Press.

Narsalay, Raghav. 2002. "The State of the Anti-Globalization Movement: Challenges Ahead." Canada Watch 9(1–2): 57–64.

National Intelligence Council, Mapping the Global Future: A Report of the National Intelligence Council's 2020 Project, Central Intelligence Agency, 2004.

National Security Archive web collection, "The Interrogation Documents: Debating U.S. Policy & Methods." http://www2.gwu.edu/~nsarchiv/NSAEBB/NSAEBB127/

New York Times, "U.S. Said to Hold More Foreigners in Iraq Fighting: Administration Calls Such Prisoners Unprotected by the Geneva Pacts," Douglas Jehl & Neil A. Lewis, January 8, 2005, pp. A1, 6.

New York Times, "Pentagon Envisioning A Costly Internet for War," Tim Weiner, November 13, 2004, A1, B2.

New York Times, "White House Fought New Curbs on Interrogations, Officials Say," Thursday, January 13, 2005, pp. A1, 16.

New York Times, "Gonzales says Humane-Policy Order Doesn't Bind CIA," Wednesday, January 19, 2005, A17.

O'Brien, R., A.M. Goetz, J.A. Scholte, and M. Williams (2000). Contesting Global Governance: Multilateral Economic Institutions and Global Social Movements. London: Cambridge University Press. Office of the Attorney General," in Mark Danner, Torture & Truth: America, Abu Ghraib, & the War on Terror, New York: New York Review of Books, 2004, pp. 92–93.

Oliveira, Francisco de. 1986. "E Agora PT'" in E Agora PT', edited by Emir Sader. Sao Paulo: Brazilense.

Ortiz, Sister Dianna, The Blindfold's Eyes: My Journey from Torture to Truth, New York: Orbis Books, 2002.

Ozai, Antonio. 1996. Partido de Massas e partido de quadros: A social-democracia e o PT. Sao Paulo: CPV – Centro de Documenta.

Palast, Greg. 2001. "Inside Corporate America." The Observer (UK). 14 October.

Panayotakis, Costas. 2001. "On the Self-Understanding of the 'Anti-Globalization' Movement: A View from Genoa," Capitalism, Nature, Socialism, vol 12(4), pp. 95–102.

Panitch, Leo. 2002. "Violence as a Tool of Order and Change: The War on Terrorism and the Antiglobalization Movement." Monthly Review. 54(2): 1–23.

Passy, Florence. 1999. "Supernational Political Opportunities As a Channel of Globalization of Political Conflicts. The Case of the Conflict Around the Rights of Indigenous Peoples." Pp. 148–169 in Social Movements in a Globalizing World, edited by D. d. Porta, H. Kriesi, and D. Rucht. New York: St. Martin's Press.

Pellow, David N. and Lisa S. Park. 2002. The Silicon Valley of Dreams: Environmental Injustice, Immigrant Workers, and the High-Tech Global Economy. New York: NYU Press.

Penniman, Nick. 2002. "Where's the Movement?" The American Prospect, vol. 13.

People's Global Action. 1998. "People's Global Action Against 'Free' Trade and the WTO," PBA Bulletin, 2(June).

Perry, Richard J. 1996. From Time Immemorial: Indigenous Peoples and State Systems. Austin: University of Texas Press.

Podobnik, B. (2001). "Globalization Protests in World-Historical Perspective," Paper presented at the annual meeting of the American Sociological Association, Anaheim, CA, August.

Polanyi, Karl. 1944. The Great Transformation: The Political and Economic Origins of Our Time. Boston: Beacon Press.

Pollin, Robert, Justine Burns and James Heintz. 2001. (Revised 2002) "Global Apparel Production and Sweatshop Labor: Can Raising Retail Prices Finance Living Wages?" Working Paper Series Number 19, Political Economy Research Institute, University of Massachusetts. Revised version accepted for Cambridge Journal of Economics.

Pontual, Pedro , and Carla Cecilia Almeida da Silva Silva. 1999. "Participa' 'o Popular nos governos petistas." Pp. 61–70 in Governo e Cidadania: Balan'o e reflex'es sobre o modo petista de governar, edited by In's Magalh'es, Luiz Barreto, and Vincente Trevas. Sao Paulo: Editora Funda' 'o Perseu Abramo.

Program on International Policy Attitudes, University of Maryland. 2000. (March 28). "Americans On Globalization: A Study of US Public Attitudes."

Prokosch, Mike and Laura Raymond. 2002. The Global Activist's Manual: Local Ways to Change the World. New York, NY: Thunder's Mouth Press.

Ratner, Steven R., "Jus Ad Bellum and Jus In Bello After September 11," American Journal of International Law, October 2002, Vol. 96, #4, pp. 905–921.

Risse, Thomas, Stephen C. Ropp, and Kathryn Sikkink, ed. 1999. The Power of Human Rights: International Norms and Domestic Change. New York:Cambridge University Press.

Ritzer, G. (1993). The McDonaldization of Society. Thousand Oaks, CA: Pine Forge Press.

Robbins, Richard H. "Anti-IMF/World Bank Protests in the Global South 1976–2001, (a partial list)," http://faculty.plattsburgh.edu/richard.robbins/legacy/Anti-IMF%20Protests%201976–2001.htm. Site viewed August 2004.

Rodrik, Dani. 1997. Has Globalization Gone Too Far? Washington, DC: Institute for International Economics.

Rose, Fred. 2000. Coalitions Across the Class Divide. Ithaca: NY: Cornell University Press.

Ross, John. 1995. Rebellion from the Roots: Indian Uprising in Chiapas. Monroe, Maine: Common Courage Press.

Ross, Robert J.S. (forthcoming). Slaves to Fashion: Poverty and abuse in the new sweat-shops. Ms. in preparation for University of Michigan Press.

Rothman, Franklin Daniel and Pamela E. Oliver. 2002. "From Local to Global: The Anti-Dam Movement in Southern Brazil 1979–1992." in Globalization and Resistance: Transnational Dimensions of Social Movements, edited by J. Smith and H. Johnston. Lanham, Md.: Rowman & Littlefield.

Rothstein: "Representative Democracy in SDS." From R. David Myers, Editor, Toward a History of the New left: Essays from within the Movement." NY: Carlson, 1989. Pp. 49–62.

Ruben, Justin. 2002. "Trading Places: Protestors Rock FTAA Meetings in Quito." In These Times.

Rucht, Dieter. 2001. "Lobbying or Protest? Strategies to Influence EU Environmental Policies," in Doug Imig and Sidney Tarrow, eds., Contentious Europeans: Protest and Politics in an Emerging Polity. Lanham, MD: Rowman & Littlefield, Ch. 6.

Rucht, Dieter & Friedhelm Neidhardt. 1999. "Methodological Issues in Collecting Protest Event Data: Units of Analysis, Sources and Sampling, Coding Problems," pp. 65–110 in: Dieter Rucht, Ruud Koopmans & Friedhelm Neidhardt (eds.) Acts of Dissent: New Developments in the Study of Protest. Lanham: Rowman & Littlefield Publishers, Inc.

Sader, Emir. 1986. E. Agora PT' Sao Paulo: Brazilense.

Sanger, David. 2001. "Using the Battle of Terrorism for Victory on Trade." The New York Times. 28 October.

Sassen, Saskia. 1998. Globalization and its Discontents. New York: The New Press.

Scher, Amy. 2001. "The Crackdown on Dissent." The Nation. 5 February: 23–26.

Schnaiberg, Allan and Gould, Kenneth A. 2000. Environment and Society: The Enduring Conflict. New York: Blackburn Press.

Scholte, Jan Aart. 2002. "The Future of Civil Society Opposition to Neoliberal Global Economic Governance." Canada Watch. 9(1–2): 59–64.

Scott, A. (1990). Ideology and the New Social Movements. London: Routledge.

Scott, James C. 1985. Weapons of the Weak: Everyday Forms of or Peasant Resistance. New Haven: Yale University Press.

Sikkink, Kathryn and Jackie Smith. 2002. "Infrastructures for Change: Transnational Organizations, 1953–1993." Pp. 24–44 in Restructuring World Politics: The Power of Transnational Agency and Norms. Sanjeev Khagram, James Riker and Kathryn Sikkink, eds. Minneapolis: University of Minnesota Press.

Silver, Beverly, and Eric Slater. 1999. "The Social Origins of World Hegemonies," in: Chaos and Governance in the Modern World System, ed. Giovanni Arrighi, Beverly Silver, Terence Hopkins, and Iftikhar Ahmad, pp. 151–240. St. Paul, MN: University of Minnesota Press.

Silver, Beverly. 1995. "World-Scale Patterns of Labor-Capital Conflict," Braudel Review, 18, pp. 155–187.

Singer, Andre. 2001. O PT. S'o Paulo: Publifolha.

Singer, P.W., Corporate Warriors: The Rise of the Privatized Military Industry, Ithaca: Cornell University Press, 2003.

Singer, P.W., "War, Profits, & the Vacuum of Law: Privatized Military Firms & International Law," Columbia Journal of Transnational Law, Spring 2004, pp. 521–549.

Sklair, Lelsie. 2002. Globalization: Capitalism and Its Alternatives, 3rd ed. Oxford: Oxford University Press.

Sklair, Leslie. 2001. The Transnational Capitalist Class. Cambridge: Blackwell.

Skocpol, Theda. 1979. States and Social Revolutions: A Comparative Analysis of France, Russia and China. New York: Cambridge University Press.

Slater, Eric. 2004 (July 4). "High Ideals Didn't Save Anti-Sweatshop Garment Factory". Los Angeles Times. B1.

Sloss, David L., "Rasul v. Bush: U.S. Supreme Court Ruling on the Availability of Federal Habeas Corpus Relief to Detainees at Guantanamo Bay Naval Base," American Journal of International Law, October 2004, Volume 98, Number 4, pp. 788–798.

Smith, Jackie. 2001. "Globalizing Resistance: The Battle of Seattle and the Future of Social Movements." Mobilization 6 (1): 1–20.

Smith, Jackie. 2002. "Bridging Global Divides? Strategic Framing and Solidarity in Transnational Social Movement Organizations," International Sociology. 17:505–528.

Smith, Jackie, Ron Pagnucco and Charles Chatfield eds. 1997. Transnational Social Movements and World Politics: Solidarity Beyond the State. Syracuse: Syracuse University Press.

Smith, Peter and Elizabeth Smythe. 1999. "Globalization, Citizenship and Technology: The MAI Meets the Internet." Canadian Foreign Policy 7(2): 83–105.

Smith, Jackie. 2002. "Bridging Global Divides? Strategic Framing and Solidarity in Transnational Social Movement Organizations." International Sociology. 17(4): 505–528.

Smith, Jackie and Hank Johnston. 2002. Globalization and Resistance: Transnational Dimensions of Social Movements. Landham, MD: Rowman and Littlefield.

Smith, Jackie. 1995. "Transnational Political Processes and the Human Rights Movement." Pp. 185–220 in Research in Social Movements, Conflict and Change, vol. 18, edited by L. Kriesberg, M. Dobkowski, and I. Walliman. Greenwood CT: JAI.

Smith, Jackie, Ron Pagnucco, and Charles Chatfield. 1997. "Transnational Social Movements and World Politics: Theoretical Framework." Pp. 59–77 in Transnational Social Movements and Global Politics: Solidarity Beyond the State, edited by J. Smith, C. Chatfield, and R. Pagnucco. Syracuse: Syracuse University Press.

Smith, Jackie. 2002. "Globalizing Resistance: The Battle of Seattle and the Future of Social Movements." Pp. 183–199 in Globalization and Resistance: Transnational Dimensions of Social Movements, edited by J. Smith and H. Johnston. Lanham, Md.: Rowman & Littlefield.

Smith, Claire Heather Burke and Graeme K. Ward. 2000. "Globalisation and Indigenous Peoples: Threat or Empowerment?" Pp. 1–24 in Indigenous Cultures in an Inter-connected World, edited by Claire Smith, and Graeme K. Ward. St. Leonards, NWS Australia: Allen & Unwin.

Snipp, C. Matthew. 1992. "Sociological Perspectives on American Indians." Annual Review of Sociology 18:351–370.

Snow, David and Robert Benford. 1988. "Ideology, Frame Resonance, and Participant

Mobilization," pp. 197–217 in Bert Klandermans, Hanspeter Kriesi, and Sidney Tarrow, eds., From Structure to Action: Comparing Social Movement Research across Cultures. International Social Movement Research, vol. 1. Greenwich, CT: JAI Press.

Snow, David and Robert Benford. 1992. "Master Frames and Cycles of Protest," pp. 135–55 in Aldon Morris and Carol Mueller eds., Frontiers in Social Movement Theory. New Haven, CT: Yale University Press.

Snow, David et al. 1986. "Frame Alignment Processes, Micromobilization, and Movement Participation." American Sociological Review. 51: 464–81.

Snow, David, E.B. Rochford, S. Warden, and Robert Benford. 1986. "Frame Alignment Processes, Micromobilization and Movement Participation." American Sociological Review 51:273–286.

Sophie. 2001. "'We Are Everywhere.' Peoples Global Action Meeting in Cochabamba, Bolivia," http://www.chiapasnews.ukgateway.net/news/020101.html,

Soule, Sarah A. 1997. "The Student Divestment Movement in the United States and tactical Diffusion: The Shantytown Protest." Social Forces 75(3): 855–883.

Steinberg, Marc. 1999. Fighting Words: working-class formation, collective action, and discourse in early nineteenth-century England Ithaca, N.Y.: Cornell University Press. Staggenborg, Suzanne. 1986. "Coalition Work in the Pro-Choice Movement: Organizational and Environmental Opportunities and Obstacles." Social Problems 33(5): 374–390.

Starr, A. (2004). "How Can Anti-Imperialism Not Be Anti-Racist? A Critical Impasse in the North American Anti-Globalization Movement." Journal of World Systems Research X (1): 119–152.

Starr, Amory. 2004. "Free Trade in the Americas," The Commoner, 9(Spring/Summer).

Stewart, Omer C. 1987. Peyote Religion: A History. Norman: University of Oklahoma Press.

Stewart, Lyle. 2001. "Getting Spooked: the Anti-globalization Movement is Gaining Momentum, but Law Enforcers are Quickly Catching Up." This Magazine 34(5): 24–8.

Stiglitz, Joseph. 2002. Globalization and Its Discontents. New York, NY: W.W. Norton and Co.

Strasburg, Jenny. 2004 (July 4). "Made In The U.S.A." The San Francisco Chronicle. J1.

Stuart, Rieky. 2003. "Last Chance for an Agreement." Toronto Globe and Mail. 30 July.

Subcomandante Marcos. 1996. Opening Remarks, First International Encuentro for Humanity and Against Neoliberalism. San Andres Sacamch'en de los Pobres, Chiapas, Mexico.

Szasz, Andrew. (1994). EcoPopulism: Toxic Waste and the Movement for Environmental Justice. Minneapolis: University of Minnesota Press. http://www.justtransition.org, accessed on 5 August 2002.

Tarrow, Sidney. 2002. "The New Transnational Contention: Organizations, Coalitions, Mechanisms." Prepared for Presentation at the Theme Panel on "Social Movements and Transnational Politics." APSA Meeting, Chicago.

Tarrow, Sidney. 1994, 1998. Power in Movement 2nd ed., New York: Cambridge University Press.

Tarrow, Sidney. Forthcoming. The New Transnational Contention: Movements, States, and Internationalization.

Tarrow, Sidney and Doug McAdam. 2003. "Scale Shift in Transnational Contention," Unpublished paper for the conference on "Transnational Processes and Social Movements" at the Villa Serbelloni, Bellagio Italy, July 22–26, 2003.

Tarrow, Sidney and Douglas Imig. 2001. Contentious Europeans: protest and politics in an emerging polity. Lanham, Md.: Rowman & Littlefield.

Tarrow, Sidney. 2001. "Transnational Politics: Contention and Institutions in International Politics." Annual Review of Political Science 4:1–20.

Taylor, B. (ed.) (1995). Ecological Resistance Movements: The Global Emergence of Radical and Popular Environmentalism. Albany: State University of New York Press.

Thanh Ha, Tu. 2003. "Police Round up WTO Protestors." Toronto Globe and Mail. 29 July.

Thornton, Russell. 1986. We Shall Live Again: the 1870 and 1890 Ghost Dance Movements as Demographic Revitalization. New York: Cambridge University Press.

Tilly, Charles. 1997. "Parliamentarization of Popular Contention in Great Britain, 1758–1834." Theory and Society 26:245–273.

Tilly, Charles. 1984. "Social Movements and National Politics." Pp. 297–317 in Statemaking and Social Movements: Essays in History and Theory, edited by C. Bright and S. Harding. Ann Arbor: University of Michigan Press.

Tilly, Charles. 1995. Popular Contention in Great Britain. Harvard University Press.

Tilly, C. (1986). The Contentious French. Cambridge, MA: Harvard University Press.

Traub-Werner, Marion. 1999. "Stop Sweatshops-Linking Workers' Struggles." Against The Current. #81 (14:3).

Trevas, Vincente. 1999. "O Partido dos Trabalhadores e suas experi'ncias de governo." Pp. 50–58 in Governo e Cidadania: Balan'o e reflex'es sobre o modo petista de governar, edited by In's Magalh'es, Luiz Barreto, and Vincente Trevas. Sao Paulo: Editora Funda''o Perseu Abramo.

Ul Haq, Mahbub, Reflections on Human Development, New York: Oxford University Press, 1995.

Union of International Associations. Annual. Yearbook of International Organizations. Brussels: Union of International Associations.

UNITE. 1998. "Commentary by UNITE on AIP "Preliminary Agreement" of 11/2/98". United Nations. 1999. Human Development Report. New York, NY: United Nations.

USAS. 2002. "New Changes to the FLA: Explanation and Renewed Criticism."

USAS. 1999. "Student Activists Nationwide Protest Corporate Sweatshop Code. Demonstrators Call On Universities To Reject Fla And Launch Nation-Wide University Anti-Sweatshop Initiative."

Van Bueren, Geraldine, ed., Childhood Abused: Protecting Children Against Torture, Cruel, Inhuman and Degrading Treatment and Punishment, Aldershot: Ashgate, 1998.

Väryrnen, R. (2000). "Anti-corporate globalization Movements at the Cross-roads."

Policy Briefs No. 4. South Bend, IN: Joan B. Kroc Institute for International Peace Studies, University of Notre Dame.

Voss, Kim and Rachel Sherman. 2000. "Breaking the Iron Law of Oligarchy: Union Revitalization in the American Labor Movement." American Journal of Sociology. 106, 2:303–349.

Wall Street Journal, "'Torture' Showdown," January 6, 2005, p. A16.

Wallace, Anthony F.C. 1969. The Death and Rebirth Of The Seneca Movement. New York: Knopf.

Wallach, Judge Evan J. http://lawofwar.org/Torture_Memos_analysis.htm

Wallerstein, Immanuel. 2002. "The United States in Decline?" Paper presented at the XXVI Political Economy of the World-System meeting, Riverside, CA, May 3.

Wallerstein, Immanuel. 2003. "Foreward." Pp. xi–xii in Emerging Issues in the 21st Century World-System: Vol. I: Crises and Resistance in the 21st World-System, edited by Wilma A. Dunaway. Westport, CT: Praeger.

Wallerstein, Immanuel. 2002. "New Revolts Against The System." New Left Review 18:29–37.

Walton, John, and David Seddon. 1994. Free Markets and Food Riots: The Politics of Global Adjustment. Cambridge, MA: Blackwell.

Wayne, Leslie. 2001. "For Trade Protestors, Slower, Sadder Songs." The New York Times. 28 October.

Weisbrot, Robert. 1990. Freedom Bound: A History of America's Civil Rights Movement. New York. Dutton.

Weller, Christian, Robert Scott and Adam Hersh. 2001. "The Unremarkable Record of Liberalized Trade." Washington, DC: Economic Policy Institute.

Welton, Neva and Linda Wolf. 2001. Global Uprising. Confronting the Tyrannies of the 21st Century. Gabriola Island, Canada: New Society Publishers.

Wickham, John A. 2002, "September 11 and America's War on Terrorism: A New Manifest Destiny." American Indian Quarterly 26:1 (Winter): 116–144.

Wilkins, David E. 2002. American Indian Politics and the American Political System. Lanham, MD: Rowman and Littlefield.

Williams, M. (2001). "In Search of Global Standards: The Political Economy of Trade and the Environment" in The International Political Economy of the Environment, edited by D. Stevis and A.J. Asetto. Boulder, CO: Lynne Rienner.

Wilmer, Franke. 1993. The Indigenous Voice in World Politics: Since Time Immemorial. Newbury Park: Sage.

Wolf, Eric. 1982. Europe and the People Without History. Berkeley: University of California Press.

World Bank. 2000. Global Economic Prospects and the Developing Countries 2000. Washington, DC: World Bank.

Index

9/11. *See* September 11, 2001

Abu Ghraib, 159
Afghanistan, U.S. invasion of, 24, 120
AFL-CIO: alliance with student
    movement of the 1990s, 118; modestly
    anti-Iraq-War stance, 121; move
    toward social movement unionism,
    127; Organizing Institute, 112;
    representation at globalization
    protests, 143n7
agricultural subsidies, division between
    developing and developed states
    over, 24n15
air inversions, 129
Aldrich, George H., 159n4
Alliance for Global Justice, 143n7
Alliance for Responsible Trade (ART),
    14
Alliance for Sustainable Jobs and the
    Environment, 137
Almeida, Tico, 112
Al Qaeda, 6, 158, 159n4, 162, 163
Alternatives for the Americas, 17
alternative summits, 16, 66
Amalgamated Clothing and Textile
    Workers Union, 112n1
American Apparel, 115n8
American Indian Movement, 98
Amnesty International, 45
"Another World Is Possible," 27
ANSWER coalition, 119
anti-colonial activism, 4
anti-corporate protests: decrease in after
    9/11, 78; in global South, 142; by
    non-governmental organizations,
    143; tactics, 77–78
anti-debt activists, 73
anti-free trade movement, 13–14
"anti-globalization," 9, 10, 20, 51. *See
    also* globalization protest movement
anti-logging campaigns, 135
anti-racism/minority rights frame, 42
anti-sweatshop movement, 111, 112–15,
    116, 118, 146

anti-toxics movement, 130
anti-war protests: in 2003 and 2004, 61;
    challenge to globalization protest
    movement collective action frame, 24;
    factional intrusion, 119; linking to
    globalization protest movement, 78;
    revival after 9/11, 24, 61, 163; in the
    U.S., 881; in Western Europe, 58
Arctic National Wildlife Refuge, 124
Argentina: austerity protests, 59–60, 61;
    economic crisis, 27; protests against
    banks, 79
Asian financial crisis of 1997, 146
Asian Social Forum, 26–27
Asia Pacific Economic and Cooperation
    (APEC), 16, 24
assimilation, 108, 109
ATTAC, 73–74, 77, 90
Auschwitz, 159n5
austerity programs, 14, 59–60, 61, 150

banks, as targets of globalization protest
    movement, 79
Belem, 89
Belgian Congo, 3
Bello, Walden, 143
Belo Horizonte, 89
Ben and Jerry's, 115
Berlusconi, Sylvio, 22n13
Bersgten, C. Fred, 142n3
Bienestar International, 115
"Big Three" globalization institutions,
    146
"Black Bloc," 144, 149n11
Black Hills, 99
blue-green coalition, 51; divergent class
    origins, 135–36; division over energy
    policy changes, 124; effect of 9/11 on,
    134–35; between environmental
    justice/anti-toxics movements,
    136–37; historical roots of, 128–30;
    problems and promise of, 131–34;
    Seattle protests not a reliable
    indicator of, 126
Blue-Green Working Group, 137

Studies in Critical Social Sciences

The Studies in Critical Social Science *book series, through the publication of original manuscripts and edited volumes, offers insights into the current reality by exploring the content and consequence of power relationships under capitalism, by considering the spaces of opposition and resistance to these changes, and by articulating capitalism with other systems of power and domination – for example race, gender, culture – that have been defining our new age.*

1. Levine, Rhonda F. (ed.). *Enriching the Sociological Imagination.* How Radical Sociology Changed the Discipline. 2004. ISBN 90 04 13992 3

2. Coates, Rodney D. (ed.). *Race and Ethnicity.* Across Time, Space and Discipline. 2004. ISBN 90 04 13991 5

3. Podobnik, Bruce and Thomas Reifer (eds.). *Transforming Globalization.* Challenges and Opportunities in the Post 9/11 Era. 2005. ISBN 90 04 14583 4

4. Pfohl, Stephen, Aimee Van Wagenen, Patricia Arend, Abigail Brooks and Denise Leckenby (eds.). *Culture, Power and History.* Studies in critical sociology. ISBN 90 04 14659 8. *In preparation*